PALEO COOKING

WITH YOUR

INSTANT POT®

80 INCREDIBLE GLUTEN- AND GRAIN-FREE
RECIPES MADE TWICE AS DELICIOUS
IN HALF THE TIME

JENNIFER ROBINS

BESTSELLING AUTHOR OF *THE NEW YIDDISH KITCHEN*,
DOWN SOUTH PALEO AND *THE PALEO KIDS COOKBOOK*

PAGE STREET
PUBLISHING CO.

PAGE STREET
PUBLISHING CO.

Copyright © 2017 Jennifer Robins

First published in 2017 by
Page Street Publishing Co.
27 Congress Street, Suite 105
Salem, MA 01970
www.pagestreetpublishing.com

Distributed by Macmillan, sales in Canada by The Canadian Manda Group.

20 19 18 17   5

ISBN-13: 978-1-62414-354-0
ISBN-10: 1-62414-354-7

Library of Congress Control Number: 2016941506

Cover and book design by Page Street Publishing Co.
Photography by Jennifer Robins

Printed and bound in China

Instant Pot® is a registered trademark of Instant Pot Company, which is not associated with this book.

Page Street is proud to be a member of 1% for the Planet. Members donate one percent of their sales to one or more of the over 1,500 environmental and sustainability charities across the globe who participate in this program.

TO MY READERS NEAR AND FAR WHO CONTINUE TO SUPPORT ME
AND WHO TRULY HAVE BECOME PART OF A COMMUNITY, NOT JUST A READERSHIP.
I APPRECIATE Y'ALL AND YOUR UNWAVERING PROFESSIONAL AND PERSONAL SUPPORT.

CONTENTS

SPEEDY SOUPS, STEWS + SAUCES 79

QUICK SIDES 117

NATURALLY SWEETENED TREATS 147

HOT BEVERAGES IN A BLINK 169

INTRODUCTION

The Paleo movement has inspired a global effort to take a look at the quality and the source of our foods and has urged us to get back into our kitchens to make our food. After decades of convenience-food offerings, cooking our food from scratch can pose several issues. First of all, why would anyone want to cook when you can pick up ready-made meals that take only minutes to prepare and consume? And second, who has the time anymore?

With increasingly busy schedules, people are overcommitted and have less downtime than ever. Even our days of rest are filled with sporting events, social occasions, weekend getaways and other commitments that leave us very little time to cook, much less cook from scratch.

When I became ill several years ago, I was housebound and mostly bedbound. I learned very quickly that in order for my body to heal, I HAD to cook. Not only was meal preparation at home a necessity, I was also limited to whole foods; so the days of microwaving easy-fix meals or tossing pasta into boiling water was a thing of the past.

Fortunately I was already a stay-at-home mom to my three children, but as I kicked off my wellness blog, Predominantly Paleo, I received massive feedback about two main issues facing those who were seeking out a Paleo lifestyle: time and money. People often feel as if they come up short with either one or the other, and the more I thought about it, the more I knew it was true. Sometimes eating whole foods can be costly and can consequently take up time, too.

Of course there are ways to work within these constructs. You can buy from farmers' markets, purchase in bulk, batch cook on the weekends, make ahead and freeze. But about a year ago I was introduced to a kitchen appliance that sort of changed the game entirely—the Instant Pot. This simply named apparatus is an electric pressure cooker with a host of other features. It can make yogurt, rice and beans (for those who consume them) and also has buttons for poultry, soups, meat/stew and chili. And it can sauté, slow cook and steam, in addition to pressure cooking, and has manual settings for when you want to wing it.

I will be honest and say that in all my life I have never wanted a pressure cooker. In fact, they've scared me. I've seen images of catastrophes that I've literally never been able to forget, and those were enough to deter me from thinking this was ever an appliance I'd own, much less use. But when I saw how simple the newer models were to operate and how safe they were, I became tempted. Temptation led to purchase. Purchase led to me trying it for the first time and forcing everyone out of the kitchen "just in case." I even shut the doors to the kitchen and warned the kids not to return to the kitchen under any circumstances until I told them it was safe to do so. True story.

But once I had my first Instant Pot experience, I was hooked. My slow cooker is collecting dust, rest its soul, and I have been using my Instant Pot multiple times a week since that first fateful day. I have experimented and played and eaten to the point that I literally had no other choice than to write a book about all that I've discovered you can do with the Instant Pot.

In this book you will find over 80 recipes, including a bone broth so simple you'll never slow-cook it again; breakfast options like an omelet packed with sautéed veggies; a jam-packed chapter of proteins for your main courses; desserts like mini chocolate Bundt cakes; and even a section with warm beverages made in minutes. I am convinced that whether you are a veteran to pressure cooking or just cracking open that IP box for the first time, you will love the versatility and wide range of options. Make sure to check out the Quick Reference Guide on page 184 to get familiar with Instant Pot settings. I have also included slow cooker options when applicable, so that those of you who are taking baby steps toward pressure cooking have options, too. I am so glad to be able to share with you the fruits of my labor. And the meats and the treats! Enjoy y'all . . . no pressure!

jen

GRAIN-FREE MORNING FARE IN A MINUTE

Breakfast in the Instant Pot? Oh, yes indeed! I am convinced that my IP hard-boiled eggs are in fact the best ever and the most efficient! Not an egg fan? That's okay, too. I will show you how to make dairy-free yogurt, breakfast cobbler and even porridge in this chapter. The days of skipping breakfast because you are in a rush are long gone—now you can eat a hearty meal on the run with these delicious pressure-cooked options!

DECKED-OUT OMELET

Though not an obvious pressure cooker recipe, I found that this omelet option is just about perfect for a college dorm or a limited kitchen setup situation. I used ghee and my eggs were perfectly fluffed and begging for delicious savory fillings. It makes a big one, so be sure to invite a friend to sit down to this four-egg wonder.

MAKES: 2 SERVINGS

4 eggs

2 tbsp (30 ml) dairy-free milk

2 tbsp (30 ml) plus 1 tsp (5 ml) ghee, olive oil, avocado oil or lard, divided

¼ cup (50 g) onion, diced

¼ cup (40 g) tomatoes, seeded and diced

3 slices bacon, cooked and crumbled

¼ cup (10 g) fresh baby spinach, chopped

Optional: ham, mushrooms, dairy-free cheese, sliced jalapeños

In a bowl whisk together your four eggs and dairy-free milk and set it aside. Warm 1 teaspoon (5 ml) of ghee or preferred cooking fat in the stainless steel bowl of your Instant Pot by pressing the Sauté button. Spoon in your diced onion and cook for about 5–8 minutes or until it softens, becomes translucent and begins to brown. Remove the cooked onions and set them aside. If you are including mushrooms in your omelet, you may sauté them at the same time as the onions and remove them accordingly. Cooking time may vary, as the mushrooms will release a lot of moisture while cooking.

Melt the remaining 2 tablespoons (30 ml) of ghee in the Instant Pot, and then press the Keep Warm/Cancel button once it's completely melted. Now pour in your egg mixture, secure the lid, close the pressure valve and press the Steam button. Press the "-" button until the display reads 5 minutes. Allow the IP to complete the cooking cycle, quick-release the pressure and remove the lid once safe to do so.

Carefully remove the cooked omelet from the bowl, using a thin flexible spatula. Transfer it to a plate and fill one half with the sautéed onion, diced tomato, bacon and spinach (or desired fillings). Then fold the other half over and serve warm.

BREAKFAST COBBLER

If you are anything like me, you need a little variety in your life. Waking up to the same breakfast day after day can be convenient and reliable, but it can get a bit boring. This breakfast cobbler is a great way to use pressure cooking in a less obvious way, and it simultaneously brings a delicious variation to your morning meal!

MAKES: 2 SERVINGS

1 pear, diced

1 apple, diced

1 plum, diced

2 tbsp (30 ml) local honey

3 tbsp (45 ml) coconut oil

½ tsp ground cinnamon

¼ cup (19 g) unsweetened shredded coconut

¼ cup (30 g) pecan pieces

2 tbsp (20 g) sunflower seeds (salted and roasted will work)

Optional garnish: Coconut whipped cream

Place your cut fruit into the stainless steel bowl of your Instant Pot. Spoon in the honey and coconut oil, sprinkle the cinnamon, secure the lid and close off the pressure valve. Press the Steam button; the display will read 10 minutes. Allow the fruit to cook, and quick-release the pressure once the cooking cycle has completed. Remove the lid once safe to do so and transfer the cooked fruit with a slotted spoon or skimmer into a serving bowl. Now place the coconut, pecans and sunflower seeds into the residual liquid and press the Sauté button. Allow the contents to cook, shifting them regularly so they do not burn. Once they are nicely browned and toasted, about 5 minutes or so, remove them and top your cooked fruit. Serve warm and topped with coconut whipped cream if desired.

ALTERNATIVE: Follow the preparations above and place the ingredients into your slow cooker accordingly. Cook on high for 1 hour and serve warm. The nuts should be topped raw; they will not toast properly in the slow cooker.

INDIVIDUAL CRUSTLESS QUICHE

I always feel like weekday breakfasts can be the hardest to conquer because of the daily hustle. Packing lunches, delivering kids to school, catching the bus or train to work or running out the door during rush hour often means we have less time to fuel our bodies. The great thing about these savory crustless quiches is you can actually make them ahead of time for the week and grab one in the morning, no labor required. To reheat, just toss one in your toaster oven for a cycle and a good solid breakfast is ready in minutes.

MAKES: 3-4 SERVINGS

1 tbsp (15 ml) ghee, olive oil or lard

⅓ cup (67 g) onion, diced

⅓ cup (22 g) freshly sliced mushrooms

3 pastured eggs

¼ cup (60 ml) dairy-free milk or water

¼ cup (10 g) baby spinach, chopped

¼ tsp onion powder

¼ tsp garlic powder

¼ tsp sea salt

Pinch black pepper

1 cup (240 ml) water

To begin, heat your ghee or preferred cooking fat by pressing the Sauté button. Toss in your onion and mushrooms and cook them for 5-8 minutes, shifting them regularly, until they are soft and beginning to brown. Remove them from the stainless steel bowl and set them aside. Now in a mixing bowl, whisk together your eggs, dairy-free milk and all of the remaining ingredients, including the sautéed onions and mushrooms.

Divide the quiche mixture into 3 or 4 individual-sized greased casserole dishes. This can be anything from a stainless steel tart pan, soufflé dish, a ceramic ramekin or a glass pan. Make sure the dishes are heat tolerant. Pour 1 cup (240 ml) of water into the IP stainless steel bowl and place the steaming rack into the bowl. Now lower your uncooked quiche pans onto the steaming rack. If you do not have room for all of them, you can actually stack them on top of each other and they will still cook through.

Secure the lid and close off the pressure valve. Press the Manual button and press the "-" button until the time reflects 10 minutes. Allow the cooking cycle to complete, and then quick-release the pressure valve and remove the lid when safe to do so. Carefully remove the mini quiches and serve warm. You can also make them ahead and refrigerate them covered. Then you can just reheat through the week and breakfast is served!

ALTERNATIVE: Follow preparation steps above, and then lower the quiche pans into your slow cooker. Cook on high for 1 hour or until cooked through.

PERFECTLY PEELABLE HARD-BOILED EGGS

Whether you love to devil them or just shake a little sea salt and pepper on them, hard-boiled eggs are versatile and the perfect "grab and go" food. If you have been looking for the most efficient way to have them ready in the fridge for your busy life, this method is the way to go!

MAKES: 6 SERVINGS

1 cup (240 ml) water

6 pastured eggs (or more or less)

Plug in your Instant Pot and pour the water in the bottom of the stainless bowl. Put in a stainless strainer/steamer basket (there is one that comes with the IP). Place your desired number of eggs on top of the opened steamer basket. Put the lid on and press the Manual button. With the "-" button, adjust it to 8 minutes on the display. Close and lock the lid and make sure the vent on top is closed. Let the IP do its magic, and then quick-release the pressure valve. Let cool slightly and vent completely before opening lid. Transfer eggs to fridge or allow to cool slightly before eating.

MEXI-EGG CUPS

These fun little egg cups are completely edible because their colorful cups are made of peppers!
This is a fantastic brunch idea and is an excellent way to pack in extra veggies. Seasoned with garlic, onion
and cumin, you can top these with chopped onion, tomatoes, avocado and lots of fresh cilantro!

MAKES: 4 SERVINGS

2 large peppers (red or green bells work well)

8 pastured eggs

1 tsp (5 g) sea salt

½ tsp onion powder

½ tsp garlic powder

¼ tsp cumin

¼ tsp ground black pepper

1 cup (240 ml) water

Optional garnishes: diced onion, tomato, avocado, salsa and cilantro sprigs

Start by slicing your peppers horizontally so that each one makes two "cups." Hollow out the interior of each to remove any seeds. Now crack two eggs into each of the pepper halves. Divide the seasonings among the 4 servings, so that each half gets a quarter of the seasonings. Now lower your Instant Pot steaming rack into the stainless steel IP bowl and pour a cup (240 ml) of water into the bottom of the bowl. Next, lower your egg-filled peppers onto the rack, placing them carefully so they do not topple over during cooking. Make a tin foil "tent" to place over the peppers so that extra water does not drip into the eggs while they are cooking. Now secure the lid and seal the pressure valve closed. Press the Manual button and then the Pressure button so that the Low Pressure light is illuminated. Now press the "-" button until 4 minutes is displayed. Allow the cooking cycle to complete, and then quick-release the pressure valve and remove the lid when safe to do so. Serve garnished with onions, tomato, avocado, fresh salsa or cilantro.

PALEO BREAKFAST PORRIDGE

Hot oatmeal or porridge is such a comforting morning meal, especially during the winter months.
In this recipe, I use a blend of nuts, seeds and coconut to make a grain-free porridge you
can make ahead in larger batches and simply reheat through the week.

MAKES: 2 SERVINGS

½ cup (55 g) cashews (raw unsalted)

¼ cup (33 g) pepitas, shelled

½ cup (60 g) pecan halves

½ cup (38 g) unsweetened dried coconut shreds

1 cup (240 ml) water

2 tsp (10 ml) coconut oil, melted

1 tbsp (15 ml) maple syrup or honey

Optional garnishes: Fresh fruit, coconut sugar or ghee

Combine all of the ingredients except for the water, coconut oil and maple syrup in a blender or food processor, and blend for around 30 seconds or until the mixture becomes a meal (like almond meal). Transfer the contents to the stainless steel bowl of your Instant Pot and stir in the water, oil and maple syrup. Secure the lid, close off the pressure valve and press the Porridge button. Now press the "-" button until the display reads 3 minutes. Allow the porridge to cook. Release the pressure valve and remove the lid once safe to do so. Stir the porridge once more and serve topped with fresh fruit, a bit of coconut sugar or ghee, if desired.

ALTERNATIVE: Follow the preparation steps above, and then place the ingredients in the slow cooker. Cook on high for 1 hour and serve warm.

CINNAMON APPLESAUCE

Applesauce is simple, soothing and a great way to start your day when you want something light and satisfying. This quick cinnamon applesauce can be made ahead, refrigerated and eaten throughout the week.

MAKES: 4 SERVINGS

5 apples, any variety

1 tbsp (8 g) ground cinnamon

½ cup (120 ml) 100% apple juice or cider

3 tbsp (21 g) grass-fed collagen powder

Core and seed apples and coarsely chop.

If using a pressure cooker or Instant Pot, place apples, ground cinnamon and juice into cooker. Secure the lid and manually select 5 minutes on high pressure. Once complete, quick-release the pressure and when appropriate, remove the lid.

When cooked, transfer contents to a blender or use an immersion blender to purée into sauce. Once smooth, add in the grass-fed collagen and stir to combine. Chill and serve.

ALTERNATIVE: If using a slow cooker, place the chopped apples, cinnamon and juice into the slow cooker and cook on low for 4 hours. Transfer the contents to a blender or use an immersion blender to purée it into sauce. Once smooth, add in the grass-fed collagen and stir to combine. Chill and serve.

BREAKFAST CASSEROLE

Pop this beauty into your Instant Pot and you've got breakfast for a week! OK, six days, but who's counting? This veggie-packed casserole is filling and perfect for on-the-go meals. If you want to add meat, sausage is the perfect companion!

MAKES: 6 SERVINGS

6 eggs

1 small sweet potato, diced

1 small onion, diced

1 yellow pepper, diced

1 tsp (5 g) sea salt

½ tsp garlic powder

½ tsp onion powder

½ tsp salt-free all-purpose seasoning

2 tbsp (30 ml) cooking fat (ghee, olive oil, avocado oil)

1 cup (240 ml) water

Optional garnish: ¼ cup (12 g) green onions, diced

Combine all of the ingredients except for the green onions in a mixing bowl and stir well. Pour the mixture into a small casserole dish (mine was 7 x 5-inches [18 x 13-cm] and glass). Now pour the water into the stainless steel bowl of your Instant Pot and lower in the steam tray. Next, lower in your filled casserole dish and make a foil "tent" so the water will deflect off while cooking. Secure the lid and close off the pressure valve. Press the Manual button and allow it to cook for the 30 minutes displayed. Quick-release the pressure valve when cooking is complete and carefully remove the lid when safe to do so. Remove the casserole dish when you are able to do so safely, and slice and serve with green onion garnish. Refrigerate indivial slices and eat throughout the week as desired.

CULTURED COCONUT MILK YOGURT

Not a fan of eggs for breakfast? No worries! This cultured coconut milk yogurt is lightly sweetened and perfectly topped with grain-free granola!

MAKES: 3 SERVINGS

2 (13.5-oz [370-ml]) cans full-fat coconut milk

3 small heat-resistant and tempered glass bowls or yogurt cups

1 tsp (5 ml) 100% vanilla extract

3 tbsp (45 ml) 100% maple syrup

2 tbsp (16 g) tapioca starch or arrowroot

1 tsp (2 g) probiotic powder (I used 200 billion cfu)

1 cup (240 ml) water

TO SERVE (OPTIONAL)

Fruit

Grain-free granola

Chill one can of coconut milk in the fridge for at least an hour. Sterilize the heat-resistant and tempered glass bowls or yogurt cups with boiling water or by running them through the dishwasher. Set them aside.

In a medium saucepan, combine one can of coconut milk, the coconut cream from the chilled can of coconut milk, vanilla and maple syrup over low heat. Stir or whisk until the cream is melted down and incorporated into the mix. Remove ¼ cup (22 g) of the mixture from the pot and whisk in the tapioca starch. Reincorporate this slurry into the heated yogurt mixture. Stir once more and then remove the saucepan from heat.

Once the yogurt mixture has cooled to around 100°F (38°C), stir in the probiotic powder. Doing so prematurely may result in killing the bacteria, destroying its ability to culture properly, so be sure to let the yogurt cool.

Now pour the water into the stainless bowl of your Instant Pot. Fill your glass bowls with the yogurt mix and place them inside the Instant Pot bowl. If your bowls do not all fit at once, you may stack them on top of each other as long as they do not spill over. Secure the lid and select the Yogurt feature. Cook for 6 hours and then remove the lid, take out the yogurt bowls, cover them and transfer them to the refrigerator to firm up further. Top with fresh fruit, grain-free granola or any other desired topping.

LEGIT BREAD UNDER PRESSURE

You may already be familiar with this recipe from online or from the *Paleo Kids Cookbook*! This method actually bakes bread in the Instant Pot, which is fantastic if you are traveling or need an alternate way to get your BLT hoppin'!

MAKES: 12 SERVINGS

¾ cup (96 g) cassava flour

¼ cup (40 g) potato starch

1 tsp (4 g) baking soda

1 tsp (4 g) sea salt

3 tbsp (28 g) psyllium husk powder (finely ground)

2 tbsp (12 g) coconut flour

7 pastured eggs

3 tbsp (45 ml) cooking fat of choice (olive oil, coconut oil, avocado oil or ghee)

1 tbsp (15 ml) apple cider vinegar

⅓ cup (113 g) local raw honey

In one mixing bowl, stir together the dry ingredients. In another bowl, combine the wet ones, stirring well to combine. Keep them separate until right before you are ready to bake. Grease a coffee canister or other vertically shaped cylinder that is safe for pressure cooking. I used a ceramic container.

Mix together the wet and dry ingredients and use an immersion blender (or regular blender) to get a smooth consistency. Immediately spoon the batter into the container you've selected, making sure it is thoroughly greased first. Now pour 3 cups (710 ml) of water into the stainless steel bowl of your Instant Pot and place your filled baking cylinder directly into the water. Grease a piece of foil and place the greased side down on top of your baking cylinder. It does not need to be fitted tightly, just secure enough to prevent water from getting inside the bread.

Next, secure the lid, close the pressure valve and press the Manual button. Then press the "+" button until 45 minutes is displayed. Allow the bread to cook. Quick-release the pressure valve and remove the lid when safe to do so.

Carefully pull the baking cylinder out and turn it upside down to release the bread. Slice and serve right away or store at room temp for a few days in an airtight container.

NOTE: The texture of this bread from the pressure cooker is denser than it is when baked. Regardless, it is a great option when traveling or during hot months, as pressure cooking uses less energy and emits less heat than an oven.

PROTEINS IN A PINCH

The hardest part about cooking a balanced meal on weeknights for most people is finding the time. People's schedules are packed with work, extracurricular activities, fitness and other commitments. One of the biggest advantages to pressure cooking is you don't have to allow hours to pull it all together. In fact, I've been known to drop the ball and forget to thaw my meat and still be able to pull off a fantastic homemade dinner by pressure cooking from frozen in minutes!

EASY GRAIN-FREE MEATBALLS

Everyone loves slow-cooked meatballs, simmering in sauce for hours—but what if you don't have that kind of time? You shouldn't have to compromise slow-cooked taste! These meatballs can be quickly thrown together after a long day and will still taste like they've been simmering all day!

MAKES: 4 SERVINGS

1 lb (454 g) grass-fed ground beef

1 pastured egg

2 tsp (10 ml) gluten-free Worcestershire sauce

1 onion, minced

1 tsp (4 g) garlic powder

1 tsp (4 g) sea salt

½ tsp ground pepper

½ tsp paprika

2 tbsp (12 g) cassava flour (almond flour and tapioca will work too)

1–2 tbsp (15–30 ml) avocado oil, ghee or olive oil

3 cups (710 ml) Bolognese (page 113) or your favorite store-bought marinara sauce

To serve: Quick Zucchini Noodles (page 140) or your favorite grain-free pasta

Combine all of the ingredients except for the cooking oil, marinara and noodles. Use your hands to mix them well, being sure to incorporate the egg, flour and seasonings thoroughly. Form golf ball–sized meatballs by hand and set them aside.

Now heat the cooking oil in the Instant Pot on the Sauté setting. Gently transfer your meatballs into the IP and brown them on all sides, being careful not to burn them. This will take up to 5 minutes total.

Pour in your Bolognese and shift the contents carefully to coat the meatballs in the sauce. Secure the lid and close the pressure valve. Press the Cancel/Off button, followed by the Manual button and then the "-" button until you decrease the displayed cook time to 8 minutes. Allow the meatballs and sauce to cook and then, when prompted, quick-release the pressure valve. Open the lid carefully when the pressure has been released and serve on top of my Quick Zucchini Noodles, on your favorite grain-free pasta noodles or just eat them alone!

ALTERNATIVE: If using a slow cooker, make the meatballs as indicated above and pour in the sauce. Place the meatballs in the sauce and cook on low for 6 hours.

SHRIMP SCAMPI

Shrimp scampi is a longtime favorite seafood dish with that buttery garlic sauce and squeeze of tangy lemon juice! If you have to ditch the dairy, have no fear, this quick pressure-cooked version gets all those yummy flavors in, taking only minutes to prepare.

MAKES: 4 SERVINGS

1 cup (240 ml) water

1 lb (450 g) tail-on frozen raw shrimp

3 tbsp (45 ml) ghee, avocado oil or olive oil

2 tsp (6 g) minced garlic

½ lemon, juiced

3 tbsp (45 ml) white wine

Sea salt to taste

¼ tsp ground black pepper

Noodles, rice or tapioca noodles, to serve

Optional garnish: fresh parsley

Begin by pouring the water into the stainless steel basin of the Instant Pot. Lower in your steamer basket (preferably one where the shrimp won't fall through the grates), and then arrange your frozen raw shrimp on top of it. Secure the lid, close off the pressure valve and press the Steam button. Now press the "-" button until the display reads 5 minutes. Once the cooking cycle is complete, quick-release the pressure valve and remove the lid when safe to do so. Remove the shrimp and pour out the water. You're ready to make the scampi sauce.

Press the Sauté button and add in your remaining ingredients, except the parsley. Stir and toss in the cooked shrimp. Shift the contents for around 2–3 minutes. Serve on noodles, rice (if tolerated) or on top of tapioca noodles. If you like your scampi extra buttery, feel free to add more ghee! Garnish with parsley.

ALTERNATIVES: If using a slow cooker, place all of the ingredients in the pot and cook on low for 3 hours. The end result may have more water content so reducing the sauce on the stovetop may be necessary.

HONEY SRIRACHA CHICKEN WINGS

I do love some good chicken wings, but sometimes I really hate the wait when they are baking. I came up with these so that if you've got some chicken in the fridge and need to whip out a game-time munchy or an on-the-spot meal, you can! This two-step process is still quicker than the time it takes to bake . . . by more than half!

MAKES: 2 SERVINGS

1 lb (450 g) pasture-raised chicken wings (or drummettes)

½ tsp sea salt

½ tsp garlic powder

¼ cup (60 ml) local honey

2 tsp (10 ml) Sriracha

2 tbsp (30 ml) cooking fat (ghee, olive oil, avocado oil)

¼ cup (60 ml) water

Start by patting your chicken wings dry with a towel. Sprinkle them with the sea salt and garlic powder. In a bowl, whisk together the honey and Sriracha. Now baste the wings with half of the honey-Sriracha mixture.

Turn your Instant Pot on and select the Sauté feature. Pour in your cooking fat and situate the chicken wings in the basin. The browning step is your only opportunity to seal in the juices and crisp the skin, so brown them on both sides (about 2 minutes on each side, being cautious not to burn), and then pour in the water and secure the lid. Close off the pressure valve and press the Keep Warm/Cancel button. Now select the Manual button and the "-" button until the time display reads 5 minutes. Once the cooking is complete, quick-release the pressure valve and remove the lid when safe. Remove the wings and drizzle with the remaining Sriracha mixture. Serve warm.

SHRIMP COCKTAIL

You know those trays you can buy with the chilled, steamed shrimp and ready-to-eat cocktail sauce? Those are pretty convenient in a pinch, but did you know you can make the same thing in about 5 minutes at home? It's true. Plus, you can choose better-quality shrimp and ingredients for that zesty cocktail sauce!

MAKES: 4 SERVINGS

1 cup (240 ml) water

1 lb (450 g) tail-on frozen raw shrimp

¼ cup (60 ml) high-quality store-bought ketchup

1 large tsp (3 g) ground fresh horseradish

1 tbsp (15 ml) coconut aminos

Squeeze of fresh lemon juice to taste

Begin by pouring the water into the stainless steel basin of the Instant Pot. Lower in your steamer basket (preferably one where the shrimp won't fall through the grates), and then arrange your frozen, raw shrimp on top of it. Secure the lid, close off the pressure valve and press the Steam button. Now press the "-" button until the display reads 5 minutes. While your shrimp steams, combine the ingredients for your cocktail sauce and stir to mix well. Once the cooking cycle is complete, quick-release the pressure valve and remove the lid when safe to do so. Immediately chill the shrimp and serve cold with the cocktail sauce.

ALTERNATIVES: Place the contents into the slow cooker and cook on low for 3 hours or until the shrimp are cooked through and pink. Chill until ready to eat while you mix your cocktail sauce.

BEEF STROGANOFF

If I can be quite honest about Stroganoff, if you had told me a few years ago that it could still be amazing without tons of sour cream and butter, I would have stared into your soul and called you a liar. And now here I am telling you that even if you can't have dairy, you will absolutely adore this recipe. And I am totally fine with you calling me a liar, because after you try it, you'll be hooked! Pinky swear!

MAKES: 8 SERVINGS

2 tbsp (30 ml) ghee, avocado oil, olive oil or preferred cooking fat

16 oz (450 g) button mushrooms, stemmed and sliced

2 onions, diced

2 lb (907 g) organic grass-fed ground beef

1 cup (240 ml) Beef Stock (page 82) or organic store-bought

1 tsp (2 g) onion powder

1 tsp (2 g) garlic powder

2 tbsp (30 ml) apple cider vinegar

1 tsp (2 g) sea salt or more to taste

1 tsp (2 g) ground black pepper

2 tbsp (30 ml) gluten-free Worcestershire sauce

2 tbsp (30 ml) high-quality ketchup

½ cup (118 ml) dairy-free milk

2 tbsp (14 g) arrowroot powder or tapioca starch

Start by pressing the Sauté button on your Instant Pot and melting the ghee or heating your preferred cooking fat. Once warm, place your sliced mushrooms and diced onions into the stainless steel IP bowl and cook them, shifting regularly to avoid burning, for about 8–10 minutes. About 5 minutes into cooking your veggies, add in your ground beef, breaking it up into crumbles as it cooks for the remaining 5 minutes. It does not have to be cooked all the way before securing the lid.

Now add in the remaining ingredients except for the dairy-free milk and arrowroot powder, which you'll reserve for last. Stir the contents, secure the lid and close the pressure valve. Press the Meat/Stew button, and then the "-" button until the display reads 15 minutes. Allow the Stroganoff to cook, and then quick-release the pressure valve. Remove the lid when safe to do so and stir the contents. In a small bowl, combine the arrowroot and dairy-free milk to make a slurry, making sure the arrowroot is completely dissolved. Now pour the milk slurry into the Stroganoff and stir. This will help it thicken a bit. Serve right away over sweet potato "noodles" or rice if tolerated.

ALTERNATIVE: If making in a slow cooker, sauté the mushrooms, onions and beef in a skillet on the stovetop before placing into the slow cooker basin. Then combine the ingredients such as above and cook on low for 4 hours or high for 2 hours.

TERIYAKI JUMBO SCALLOPS

You know those beautiful, sophisticated jumbo sea scallops you like to order in restaurants but wouldn't dare try making yourself for fear of messing them up? Well I'm here to report you can make them at home and make them a complete success! This method yields fantastically tender scallops with a savory teriyaki-inspired sauce. No more worries; you got this!

MAKES: 3 SERVINGS

1 tbsp (15 ml) avocado oil

1 lb (450 g) jumbo sea scallops, fresh or thawed from frozen

½ cup (118 ml) coconut aminos

3 tbsp (45 ml) 100% maple syrup

½ tsp garlic powder

½ tsp ground ginger

½ tsp sea salt

To garnish: Fresh minced chives

To begin, pour your tablespoon (15 ml) of avocado oil into the stainless steel bowl and press the Sauté button on your Instant Pot. Sear the scallops for about a minute on each side. While they cook, quickly whisk together your remaining ingredients, leaving the chives out to use as a garnish. Pour the sauce over the scallops and secure the lid. Press the Warm/Cancel button and secure the pressure valve. Now press the Steam button, and then the "-" button until the display reads 2 minutes. Allow the scallops to steam. Quick-release the pressure valve and remove the lid once safe to do so. Remove the scallops and set aside. If your sauce is too thin, simply press the Sauté button and allow the sauce to reduce, usually taking only a few minutes. If you wish to serve with a thinner sauce, ladle the sauce, as is, over your scallops. Serve with minced chives to garnish.

ALTERNATIVE: If making in a slow cooker, combine all of the ingredients and cook on high for 30–35 minutes. The sauce may need to be reduced in a saucepan or on the stovetop if too thin.

BACON TURKEY MEATLOAF

People tend to love meatloaf or leave it, but I for one think it is absolutely fantastic—if done right!
It's all about flavor and texture and making sure you don't overcook and under-season, which is why this
Instant Pot version with sautéed onions and bacon knocks it out of the park!

MAKES: 4 SERVINGS

FOR THE MEATLOAF

1 cup (240 ml) water

1 onion, diced and sautéed

1 lb (450 g) pastured ground turkey meat

3 strips cooked crisped bacon, chopped

¼ cup (60 ml) high-quality store-bought
ketchup

1 tsp (5 g) garlic sea salt

½ tsp black pepper

1 egg

¼ cup (24 g) cassava flour, arrowroot,
almond flour or preferred grain-free flour

FOR THE TOPPING

¼ cup (60 ml) high-quality store-bought
ketchup

1 tbsp (15 ml) apple cider vinegar

1 tbsp (15 ml) 100% maple syrup

3 strips cooked crisped bacon, chopped

Begin by pouring the cup (240 ml) of water into the stainless steel Instant Pot bowl. Lower in the steamer rack. To assemble the meatloaf, combine all of the remaining meatloaf ingredients in a mixing bowl and mix by hand. Tear off a sheet of foil and form a loaf out of your meat mixture, placing it onto the foil sheet. Wrap up your uncooked meatloaf, securing the foil around the edges. This will help keep your meat insulated and also protect it from breaking apart as it cooks.

Now lower the foil-wrapped meatloaf onto the steamer rack. Secure the lid and close the pressure valve. Press the Meat/Stew button on your Instant Pot, and then press the "-" button until 20 minutes is displayed. Allow the meatloaf to cook. While it does, mix together your ketchup, apple cider vinegar and maple syrup. You can choose to heat it a bit in a saucepan over low heat on the stovetop for about 5 minutes or keep it as is. Warming it will help the flavors merge that much better.

Once the meatloaf has completed cooking, quick-release the pressure valve and remove the lid once safe to do so. Carefully remove the foil-wrapped meatloaf once it's cool enough to handle and unwrap it. Spoon the sauce over the top of the meatloaf and sprinkle with the remaining chopped bacon. Slice and serve right away.

NOTE: You may choose to cook your onion and/or bacon in the Instant Pot prior to cooking the meatloaf. You can use the Sauté feature for both options, using a bit of cooking fat for the onion, and sautéing for around 10 minutes. The bacon can be cooked without additional fat on the Sauté feature for about 10 minutes or until desired crispness has been reached.

ALTERNATIVE: You can cook this meatloaf in the slow cooker wrapped in foil for about 3-4 hours on low or in about 2 hours on high. Simply follow the directions above and once wrapped in foil, place it directly into the slow cooker basin and set it accordingly. Water in the basin is not necessary.

VEGGIE STUFFED EGGPLANT

You know that feeling when you just want a gigantic salad packed with every veggie you can imagine? Like your body is screaming for nutrients and is so happy when you reward it with them? Well that is sort of the story with this stuffed eggplant. It's packed with tons of savory plants, good fats and is filling even without meat. And it takes about 10 minutes to pull together, which is even more fantastic.

MAKES: 2 SERVINGS

1 large eggplant, sliced lengthwise

4 tbsp (60 ml) avocado oil or olive oil, divided

2 tsp (10 g) garlic sea salt

2 tbsp (30 ml) water

¼ cup (50 g) carrots, diced

1 onion, diced

1 zucchini, diced

3 cloves garlic, minced

1 tsp (5 g) sea salt

1 tsp (2 g) onion powder

1 cup (240 ml) marinara

To garnish: 2 tbsp (8 g) roasted salted pumpkin seeds (pepitas)

To prepare your eggplant, score the fleshy sides with a knife, making a grid pattern. Then drizzle 1 tablespoon (15 ml) of oil on each half and sprinkle each half with 1 teaspoon (5 g) of garlic sea salt. Now drizzle 1 more tablespoon (15 ml) of oil into the stainless steel bowl of your Instant Pot and add in the 2 tablespoons (30 ml) of water. Place the eggplant halves fleshy side down and secure the lid to your IP. Press the Manual button, and then the "-" button until 5 minutes is displayed. Close the pressure valve and allow the eggplant to cook. Once the cycle is complete, release the pressure valve and remove the lid once safe to do so. Remove the eggplant halves and place them fleshy-side up on a serving plate.

Add in your remaining veggies and seasonings and drizzle with the remaining tablespoon (15 ml) of cooking oil. Press the Keep Warm/Cancel button, and then the Sauté button. Stir the vegetables continually, allowing them to soften, about 5–7 minutes. Add in the marinara sauce and stir for 2 more minutes to heat through. Now spoon the vegetable mixture into the eggplant halves, sprinkle each half with a tablespoon (4 g) of pumpkin seeds and serve warm.

ZESTY CITRUS PULLED CHICKEN

When I made this recipe, I was excited to have another chicken dish in my arsenal for busy weeknights, but I never anticipated how much my family would love it! This was a crowd pleaser to such a degree that we ran out and everyone was still asking for more!

MAKES: 4 SERVINGS

1 tbsp (15 ml) cooking fat (avocado oil, olive oil or ghee)

1 lb (450 g) pastured organic boneless chicken breasts

½ cup (118 ml) organic orange juice

2 tsp (10 ml) gluten-free Worcestershire sauce

1 heaping tsp (2 g) garlic powder

1 tsp (5 g) sea salt

½ tsp chili powder

½ tsp paprika

To serve: Grain-free tortillas or salad greens

Begin by drizzling the cooking fat into the Instant Pot basin. Place the chicken on top of the oil. Combine the remaining ingredients in a bowl and pour over the chicken. Secure the Instant Pot lid and close the pressure valve. Press the Poultry button and allow the chicken to cook (15 minutes). If cooking from frozen you will need to increase cooking time by approximately 5–10 minutes. Once complete, quick-release the pressure valve and remove the lid when safe. Shred the chicken with two forks. Serve on grain-free tortillas or on top of salad greens.

ALTERNATIVE: If using a slow cooker, add all of the ingredients and cook on low for 4–5 hours or until the chicken is cooked through and easy to shred.

PRESSURE-COOKED SIRLOIN STEAK

So it's the dead of winter and you can't stand the thought of grilling outdoors. Or you don't even have a grill but have a hankering for a juicy steak. Or maybe you dwell in a studio apartment and don't even have a full kitchen. This is the recipe for you. These deliciously juicy steaks are done in minutes and are outstanding!

MAKES: 2 SERVINGS

2 (10 oz [284 g]) grass-fed sirloin steaks (or preferred cut)

¼ cup (60 ml) red wine

¼ cup (60 ml) coconut aminos

3 tbsp (45 ml) cooking fat (olive oil, ghee, avocado oil), divided

3 tbsp (45 ml) gluten-free Worcestershire

1 tsp (2 g) garlic powder

1 tsp (2 g) onion powder

1 tsp (2 g) black pepper

1 tsp (5 g) sea salt

1 tsp (2 g) paprika

Juice from 1 lemon

In a zip-top bag, combine the steaks, wine, aminos, 2 tablespoons (30 ml) cooking fat, worcestershire, garlic powder, onion powder, pepper, salt, paprika and lemon. Give the bag a good shake to coat the steaks and refrigerate until ready to cook. I let mine marinate for 3 hours, but you could go overnight or less time if needed. Turn on your Instant Pot and drizzle in the remaining 1 tablespoon (15 ml) of cooking oil. Press the Sauté button and allow it to preheat for a minute or two.

Gently transfer the steaks to the IP basin and sear on each side for 1 minute per side. Pour in the remaining marinade and secure the lid. Close the pressure release valve and press the Warm/Cancel button to turn the IP off. Now press the Manual button, and then press the "-" button until you decrease the time display to read 4 minutes. This will yield a medium steak, with some pink in the middle. If you choose to cook longer, you can reduce the amount of pink, but keep in mind the longer you cook a sirloin, the tougher it can be.

Next, quick-release the pressure valve and allow the steam to escape. Remove the lid once safe to do so and remove the steaks. Salt and pepper to taste. You can spoon some of the remaining juices over them and serve right away.

ALTERNATIVE: If using a slow cooker, place the steaks (you can use alternative cuts of meat as well) in the bottom of the slow cooker basin and pour the marinade (including the second tablespoon [15 ml] of oil) on top of the steaks. Allow the steaks to cook on low for approximately 4 hours or until cooked to desired doneness.

CILANTRO CHICKEN MEATBALLS

These simple meatballs come together quickly enough for a weeknight dinner, yet they are scrumptious enough to serve to a party of special guests! You'll love the combination of garlic and onion with the subtle undertone of sesame oil and fresh cilantro.

MAKES: 4 SERVINGS

1 lb (450 g) ground pastured chicken

½ onion, minced

2 tbsp (30 ml) sesame oil

½ cup (20 g) fresh cilantro, chopped

1 egg

¼ cup (60 ml) coconut aminos

2 tbsp (30 ml) apple cider vinegar

1 tsp (5 g) sea salt

½ tsp garlic powder

¼ cup (60 ml) avocado oil, olive oil or preferred cooking fat

¼ cup (60 ml) water

To assemble the meatballs, begin by combining all of the ingredients, except for the cooking fat and water, in a mixing bowl. Use your hands to make sure the ingredients are incorporated well with each other.

Plug in your Instant Pot, pour the ¼ cup (60 ml) cooking fat into the stainless steel basin and press the Sauté button. Shape your meatballs until they are a couple of inches (5 cm) in diameter and place them into the hot oil. Cook the meatballs on all sides until they begin to brown, around 5 minutes, and then press the Warm/Cancel button. Add the water into the bottom of the stainless bowl. Secure the lid to the IP, close off the pressure valve and press the Manual button. Now press the "-" button until the display reads 5 minutes.

Allow the meatballs to cook. Once complete, quick-release the pressure valve and remove the lid once safe to do so. Transfer the meatballs onto a towel-lined plate and serve warm.

ALTERNATIVE: These can be made in the slow cooker. Follow the initial directions above, shaping the raw ingredients, and then place the uncooked meatballs into the slow cooker basin. Cook on low for 3–4 hours or high for around 1–2 hours. You will want to omit the water in the cooking basin but should include a bit of oil to prevent sticking.

INSTANT POT ROAST

I do love a good pot roast, but the preparation time is unnerving. I want that slow-cooked, tender, juicy pot roast that can often take all day to get right, but in a fraction of the time. Once I figured out how to pressure-cook it to perfection, I was pretty excited and so was my carnivorous husband! Be sure to adjust the cooking times on this one if you use a bigger roast!

MAKES: 4 SERVINGS

1 tbsp (15 ml) avocado oil, olive oil or preferred cooking fat

1 large onion, sliced into rings

2 lb (907 g) grass-fed beef roast

1 lb (450 g) carrots

1 lb (450 g) small gold potatoes

24 oz (680 ml) Beef Stock (page 82)

1 tsp (5 g) sea salt

½ tsp ground black pepper

1 tsp (2 g) onion powder

2 tbsp (30 ml) coconut aminos or gluten-free Worcestershire sauce

3 tbsp (18 g) arrowroot, tapioca or cassava flour

Fresh thyme (optional)

Start by pressing the Sauté button on your Instant Pot and drizzling in your cooking fat. Place the onion slices into the oil and cook for around 5 minutes, shifting them so they do not burn. Now move your onions to the side and place the roast into the stainless steel pot, searing on each side for about 2 minutes per side. Place the rest of the veggies into the pot and pour the broth over them. Add in the seasonings and coconut aminos and stir to combine. Now press the Keep Warm/Cancel button, secure the lid and close the pressure valve. Next, press the Manual button, and then the "+" button until 65 minutes is displayed.

Allow the cooking cycle to complete. Quick-release the pressure valve and remove the lid when safe to do so. Remove the vegetables and roast from the Instant Pot and transfer them to a serving platter. Now you'll want to thicken the gravy. To do this, remove about ¼ of a cup (60 ml) of the broth from the bowl and whisk in 3 tablespoons (18 g) of arrowroot to that reserved broth. Once it's combined, stir the slurry back into the pot to thicken your gravy; this will take a couple minutes of stirring gently. Ladle the thickened gravy over your roast and veggies and serve right away. Garnish with fresh thyme if desired.

ALTERNATIVE: If you prefer to make it in a slow cooker, combine all of the ingredients in the slow cooker except for the arrowroot. Turn the slow cooker on low for 7–8 hours, then when cooked through, remove all of the meat and veggies and follow the remaining directions above.

CHICKEN TIKKA MASALA

The first time I was introduced to Indian food, I ate tikka masala and thought it was absolutely amazing. To this day it is still my favorite, especially knowing how easy it is to make at home without dairy or grain. Of course you can serve this over basmati rice, if you tolerate gluten-free grains; otherwise, cauliflower or zucchini "rice" are both great options!

MAKES: 4 SERVINGS

1 lb (450 g) chicken breast or thighs, cut into bite-sized pieces

1 large onion, diced

1 tsp (3 g) minced garlic

¼ tsp ginger

1–2 tsp (3–5 g) garam masala

2 tsp (5 g) paprika

28 oz (765 ml) organic crushed tomatoes (jarred)

1 tsp (2 g) turmeric

2 tsp (10 g) sea salt

2 tbsp (30 ml) tomato paste

1 tsp (2 g) cumin

½ tsp cinnamon

1 cup (240 ml) full-fat coconut milk

To serve: Your favorite grain-free rice and fresh cilantro

Combine all of the ingredients except for the coconut milk, rice and cilantro in the stainless steel bowl of your Instant Pot. Give them a quick stir to make sure the seasonings are incorporated and the chicken is submerged. Secure the lid, close off the pressure valve and press the Poultry button. You will see 15 minutes displayed. Allow the cooking cycle to finish. Quick-release the pressure valve and remove the lid once safe to do so. Your IP will automatically switch over to its warming feature once complete. You can leave it on this setting as you stir in your full fat coconut milk. Once the milk has been incorporated, you can serve it on top of cauliflower rice, basmati rice (if tolerated) or zucchini rice, my favorite grain-free rice alternative. Top with fresh cilantro.

ALTERNATIVE: In a slow cooker add all of the ingredients except for the coconut milk. Stir and cook on low for 6 hours or high for 3 hours. At the last 30 minutes, add the coconut milk. Stir and then serve over zucchini rice, cauliflower rice or basmati rice if tolerated. Top with fresh cilantro. If the sauce is too thin, consider reducing it on the stovetop or thickening it with a couple of tablespoons of tapioca starch.

BBQ BEEF SHORT RIBS

Those of you who know me know that, as a Texas girl, BBQ is near and dear to me. However, living on the East Coast means that I have experienced lots of disappointment when it comes to authentic grub. I don't make BBQ at home all the time, but I must say this recipe was the perfect way to cure a craving!

MAKES: 2 SERVINGS

8 oz (227 g) short ribs

Sea salt and pepper

3 tsp (15 ml) olive oil, avocado oil or lard

1 large onion, sliced into rings

½ cup (118 ml) high-quality store-bought ketchup

½ cup (118 ml) crushed tomatoes

¼ cup (60 ml) local honey

½ tsp onion powder

1 tsp (5 ml) liquid smoke

½ tsp garlic powder

½ tsp sea salt

Optional: 1 tsp (5 ml) gluten-free Worcestershire sauce

Fresh thyme, optional

To serve: Potato Salad (page 131) and Steamed Greens + Bacon (page 135)

First season your short ribs with sea salt and pepper. Drizzle the cooking oil into the stainless steel bowl and press the Sauté button. After the oil heats, around a minute or so, transfer the seasoned ribs and onions into the oil. Cook the ribs on each side for about 3 minutes. Combine the ketchup, tomatoes, honey, onion powder, liquid smoke, garlic powder, sea salt and Worcestershire sauce in a bowl and stir. Now pour the sauce over the ribs, secure the lid and close the pressure valve. Press the Manual button, and then the "-" button until the display reads 28 minutes. Allow the cooking cycle to complete. Quick-release the pressure valve and remove the lid once safe to do so.

Remove the ribs from the sauce, which will become quite oily. Ladle off as much of the fat as you wish to before reducing the BBQ sauce. It's okay to leave a little fat. Now press the Sauté button once more and allow the sauce to simmer for about 10 minutes. As it reduces, the onions and sauce could potentially stick to the bottom of the stainless steel bowl, so use a spoon to shift the contents if this begins to happen. Once the sauce has reached your desired texture and thickness, spoon it on top of the ribs and serve. Garnish with fresh thyme if desired. This dish is great paired with my Potato Salad and my Steamed Greens + Bacon.

ALTERNATIVE: If using a slow cooker, place all of the ingredients except for the cooking fat in the slow cooker basin and cook on low for 8 hours or high for 4 hours. Remove the ribs and ladle off any fat from the top of the sauce remaining in the slow cooker. Once you've ladled the desired amount of fat off, purée the sauce using an immersion blender or, alternatively, transfer it to a blender and purée. Serve ribs with the sauce and aforementioned side dish options.

ROTISSERIE CHICKEN

This is one of those recipes I hesitate to even call a recipe! It's so easy you could do it blindfolded. Although in the name of safety, let's cook this juicy, seasoned bird with all of our senses intact, shall we? Good plan!

MAKES: 4 SERVINGS

1 whole chicken, 3–4 lb (1.4–1.8 kg)
1 tsp (5 g) sea salt
1 tsp (2 g) ground black pepper
1 tsp (2 g) paprika
½ tsp garlic powder
½ tsp onion powder
1 tsp (2 g) salt-free, all-purpose seasoning
2 cups (303 g) chopped carrots
1 onion, diced
1 tbsp (15 ml) olive oil, avocado oil or ghee

Simply place the whole chicken into the Instant Pot and sprinkle with salt, pepper, paprika, garlic powder, onion powder and all-purpose seasoning. Place your vegetables around the chicken and drizzle them with your cooking fat. Secure the lid and close off the pressure valve. Press the Poultry button and then the "+" button until the display reads 25 minutes. Allow the chicken to cook and then quick-release the pressure valve when the cooking cycle is complete. Remove the lid when safe to do so. Serve warm.

ALTERNATIVE: If using a slow cooker, place all of the ingredients into the slow cooker, drizzle the cooking fat over your veggies, cover and cook the chicken on low for 4–6 hours, or until the chicken is cooked through. The meat will fall off the bone once cooked and sliced.

PARCHMENT-WRAPPED SALMON

Can you keep a secret? I am not a huge salmon fan. I know, "everybody" loves it and it's so good for us, but I just never fell in love with it the way so many others have. Even my 9-year-old son is obsessed! So basically my goal was this: Make a salmon recipe that is not too fussy but will make me like it. And I think I did it!!! So far I am loving this parchment-wrapped salmon right out of the pressure cooker. The glaze is made of just four ingredients, a mix of savory and sweet, and I have a strong suspicion I'll be making this again and again!

MAKES: 3 SERVINGS

3 tbsp (45 ml) stone-ground mustard

2 tbsp (30 ml) local honey

1 tsp (3 g) minced garlic

1 tbsp (15 ml) coconut aminos

3 wild-caught salmon fillets
(about ⅓ lb [150 g] each, fresh or thawed from frozen)

1 cup (240 ml) water

Sea salt to taste

Fresh thyme (optional)

Start by mixing the mustard, honey, garlic and coconut aminos together in a small bowl. Next, poke holes in the fleshy side of the salmon and spoon ⅓ of the glaze over each of the fillets. Take 3 pieces of parchment paper and wrap them so that the fillets are each encapsulated but the parchment does not rub the glaze off. Now pour 1 cup (240 ml) water into the stainless steel bowl of your Instant Pot. Lower in your steaming rack and place the wrapped fillets on top of the steaming rack—next to each other if possible as opposed to being stacked. Secure the lid, close the pressure valve, press the Manual button and then the "-" button until 5 minutes is displayed. Allow the cooking cycle to complete, and then quick-release the pressure valve. Remove the lid once safe to do so, and then carefully remove the parchment-wrapped salmon. Serve warm. If desired, you may make additional sauce and garnish with fresh thyme.

ALTERNATIVE: Follow the preparations above. Lower your parchment-wrapped salmon into your slow cooker and cook on low for 1–2 hours or until cooked through.

CARNITAS

Restaurant carnitas can be intimidating to an average "home cook," but they need not be!
Pressure-cooked carnitas take a lesser cut of meat and turns it into the most delicious savory
shredded pork, perfect for rolling up in a homemade, grain-free tortilla!

MAKES: 4 SERVINGS

1 (2 lb [907 g]) pastured pork loin

1 cup (240 ml) water

1 orange, sliced in half

1 fresh jalapeño, whole

1 large red onion, diced

2 tsp (10 g) sea salt

1 tsp (2 g) cumin

1 tsp (2 g) onion powder

1 tsp (2 g) garlic powder

½ tsp black pepper

1 tsp (1 g) dried parsley

1 tsp (2 g) paprika

Handful fresh cilantro

To serve: Cilantro, diced tomato, onion
and jalapeño slices

Place all of the ingredients into the stainless steel bowl of your Instant Pot, squeezing the juice from the orange halves before placing them into the bowl. Secure the lid, close off the pressure valve and press the Meat/Stew button. Now press the "+" button until 40 minutes is displayed. Allow the cooking cycle to complete, and then allow the pressure to release slowly. Remove the lid when safe to do so and use two forks to shred the pork. You may need to adjust the cooking time if the weight of your meat varies. Serve with more fresh cilantro, diced tomato, onion and jalapeño slices if desired.

ALTERNATIVE: Place all of the ingredients into your slow cooker, omitting the water. Squeeze the oranges to juice them over the meat before placing them into the slow cooker. Cook on low for 8 hours. Shred the meat with two forks before serving.

LEMON GARLIC CHICKEN

This very simple recipe is also full of flavor—not too sophisticated, and just the right balance of lemon, garlic and tender chicken breast. And since it takes only 20 minutes in the Instant Pot, it's a great option when you are out of ideas AND time!

MAKES: 4 SERVINGS

1 onion, diced

1 tbsp (15 ml) avocado oil, lard or ghee

4 pasture-raised chicken breasts (or sub thighs)

1 tsp (5 g) sea salt

5 garlic cloves, minced

½ cup (118 ml) organic Chicken Stock (page 81) or high-quality store-bought

1 tsp (1 g) dried parsley

¼ tsp paprika

¼ cup (60 ml) white cooking wine

1 large lemon juiced (or more to taste)

3-4 tsp (6-8 g) (or more) arrowroot flour

Turn your Instant Pot to the Sauté feature and place in the diced onion and cooking fat.

Cook the onions for 8-10 minutes or until softened and nicely browned. Add in the remaining ingredients except for the arrowroot flour and secure the lid on your Instant Pot.

Select the Poultry setting (15 minutes) and make sure your pressure valve is closed.

Allow cook time to complete. Release the pressure valve to vent and carefully remove the lid. At this point you may thicken your sauce by making a slurry. To do this, remove about ¼ cup (60 ml) of sauce from the pot, add in the arrowroot flour, whisking well, and then reintroduce the slurry into the remaining liquid. Stir and serve right away. This also reheats well as leftovers.

ALTERNATIVE: Combine all of the ingredients except arrowroot in your slow cooker. Cook on low for 4 hours. Follow the steps above to thicken the sauce with the arrowroot powder.

HONEY BALSAMIC PORK CHOPS

Pork chops can often yield a texture that is tough, not tender. Turns out pressure-cooking them is a great way to get the desired texture and flavor without compromising either. This honey balsamic combo has a savory kick you'll love!

MAKES: 4 SERVINGS

4 pork chops (boneless or bone-in, ¾-inch [2-cm] thick)
Sea salt and pepper to taste
¼ cup (60 ml) ghee
½ cup (118 ml) local honey
½ cup (118 ml) balsamic vinegar
1 tbsp (10 g) minced garlic
1 tsp (1 g) dried parsley

Season your pork chops with sea salt and pepper. Melt ghee in the stainless steel pot of your Instant Pot using the Sauté feature. Sear the pork chops on each side for 1 minute. Add in the remaining ingredients, press the Keep Warm/Cancel button and stir. Secure the lid, close the pressure valve and press the Poultry button (high pressure, 15 minutes). Allow the cooking cycle to complete. Quick-release the pressure valve and remove the lid when safe to do so. Serve warm.

ALTERNATIVE: Combine all of the ingredients in a slow cooker and cook on high for 4 hours.

SALAD TOPPER TURKEY FILLETS

I wrote this recipe as a quick alternative to the infamous "grilled chicken" salad topper. Of course you don't have to place these on a salad; they are delicious on top of Quick Zucchini Noodles (page 140) or straight out of the pressure cooker!

MAKES: 4 SERVINGS

4 turkey breast fillets

¼ cup (60 ml) olive oil or avocado oil

1 tsp (5 g) sea salt or more to taste

¼ cup (60 ml) orange or lemon juice

1 tbsp (10 g) minced garlic

¼ cup (60 ml) coconut aminos

1 tbsp (2 g) dried tarragon

1 tbsp (2 g) dried parsley

To serve: Salad greens or veggies

Combine all of the ingredients in a zip-top bag and marinate in the refrigerator for 1 hour or more. Pour entire contents of the bag into the stainless steel bowl of your Instant Pot and secure the lid. Close off the pressure valve and press the Poultry button (high pressure, 15 minutes). Allow the cooking cycle to complete. Quick-release the pressure valve and remove the lid when safe to do so. Remove the turkey fillets and serve atop salad greens or with desired veggies.

ALTERNATIVE: Follow preparations above except place contents in the slow cooker. Cook on high for 3 hours or until cooked through. Serve atop salad greens or with desired veggies.

CREAMY BUFFALO CHICKEN LEGS

This ain't your average chicken y'all! It's got kick and pizazz and just the right balance of creamy sauce to zesty spice! My kids loved this one!

MAKES: 4 SERVINGS

4 bone-in pastured chicken legs

Sea salt and pepper to taste

2 tbsp (30 ml) ghee

1 onion, diced

2 tbsp (30 ml) high-quality store-bought mayonaise

3 tbsp (45 ml) gluten-free hot wing sauce (high-quality store-bought)

¼ cup (60 ml) Chicken Stock (page 81)

2–3 tbsp (12 g) arrowroot or tapioca

Begin by patting your chicken dry and sprinkling it with sea salt and pepper to taste. Now melt the ghee in the stainless steel bowl of your Instant Pot by pressing the Sauté button. Once the ghee is melted, place the chicken legs skin-side down, and allow them to cook for around 6 minutes or until the skin begins to crisp. Pressure cooking will not yield crispy skin, so this step is useful in preventing the skin from becoming too soft.

Once you've gotten your skin crispy (cooking both sides to desired texture), toss in your diced onions for a few minutes before adding the mayo, hot wing sauce and chicken stock. Stir those remaining ingredients in the IP (reserving the arrowroot for later) and secure the lid. Close the pressure valve and press the Poultry button, which will cook the chicken at high pressure for 15 minutes. Next, quick-release the pressure valve after the cooking cycle has completed and remove the lid. Carefully remove the chicken from the pot; now you can thicken your sauce. To do this, remove ¼ cup (60 ml) of the sauce and whisk in the arrowroot starch (or tapioca). Now stir the slurry back into the main pot until the sauce thickens, after a minute or so. Serve right away and spoon sauce over the top of the chicken legs.

STUFFED CABBAGE ROLLS

This old favorite has a few "hands-on" steps that make it sort of cumbersome, at least for a simple weeknight meal. I've tried to shorten the time so that this yummy dish can be made anytime and not just for special occasions. The tangy tomato sauce is the perfect pairing with the beef and cauliflower rice enveloped in cabbage leaves.

MAKES: 10 SERVINGS

1 cup (240 ml) water

1 head cabbage (you will use about 10 of the leaves, double remaining ingredients if you want to make more)

1 lb (450 g) grass-fed ground beef

1 egg

1 cup (210 g) uncooked cauliflower rice

¼ cup (60 ml) coconut milk

1 onion, minced

1 tsp (5 g) sea salt

1 tsp (2 g) onion powder

1 tsp (2 g) garlic powder

14 oz (383 ml) tomato sauce

1 tbsp (15 ml) lemon juice

2 tbsp (30 ml) gluten-free Worcestershire sauce or coconut aminos

2 tbsp (24 g) maple sugar or coconut palm sugar

1 tbsp (6 g) arrowroot or tapioca

Start by softening the cabbage leaves. To do this, pour the water into the stainless steel bowl of your Instant Pot and lower in the steaming rack. Place the head of cabbage onto the rack, secure the lid and close the pressure valve. Now press the Steam button, and then the "-" button until 5 minutes is displayed. Allow the cabbage to steam. Quick-release the pressure valve and remove the lid once safe to do so. Remove the cabbage and discard the water.

While your cabbage steams, combine the raw meat, egg, cauliflower rice, coconut milk, onion, salt, onion powder and garlic powder in a mixing bowl. Combine by hand until ingredients are incorporated well with each other.

In another small bowl, mix the tomato sauce, lemon juice, Worcestershire sauce and maple sugar, stirring to combine. Peel apart the cabbage leaves, carefully so they do not tear. Now take about ⅒ of the meat mixture and roll it up into a cabbage leaf, wrapping it like a burrito so all sides are tucked neatly underneath. Repeat until all of the meat is used. Place them carefully, but snugly, into the IP bowl. Pour the tomato sauce mixture on top.

Secure the lid, close the pressure valve and press the Poultry button. This will automatically cook the cabbage rolls on high pressure for 15 minutes. Quick-release the pressure once complete and remove the lid. Now you may thicken the sauce with 1 tablespoon (6 g) of arrowroot starch or tapioca. To do this, make a slurry by removing ¼ cup (60 ml) of the tomato sauce and whisking in the tapioca or arrowroot. Now stir the slurry back into the main pot, allowing it to thicken while you stir for a minute or so. Serve right away, ladling sauce over the top of the rolls.

ALTERNATIVE: Soften the cabbage leaves in hot water until you can easily remove them without cracking. Now combine the raw meat, egg, cauliflower rice, coconut milk, onion, salt, onion powder and garlic powder in a mixing bowl. Combine by hand until ingredients are incorporated well with each other. In another small bowl, mix the tomato sauce, lemon juice, Worcestershire sauce and maple sugar, stirring to combine. Carefully peel apart the cabbage leaves and take ⅒ of the meat mixture and roll it up into a cabbage leaf, like a burrito. Repeat until all of the meat is used. Place them carefully, but snugly, into the slow cooker. Pour the tomato sauce mixture on top. Cook on low for 8 hours, serve warm.

SPEEDY SOUPS, STEWS + SAUCES

Nothing is quite as comforting as a piping hot bowl of soup or stew. You can make it rich and hearty or light and broth based, but it always hits the spot. With a pressure cooker, you can make all of your favorites in a fraction of the time as slow cooking, yet yield the same savory results.

I personally love that I can reduce my cook time for homemade bone broth drastically, so that I can make multiple batches in a day and store for later! So make some ahead, freeze it or give some to a friend. Being able to whip up a fresh batch so quickly will help keep bellies warm all year round!

CHICKEN STOCK

Making homemade chicken stock is not only cost effective, it's more nutrient dense and delicious than store-bought stock. I like to pressure-cook a whole pasture-raised chicken, and then I remove the meat and make the stock right away. You can repeat making batches of stock until the bones become brittle. Freeze the excess for later!

MAKES: 10 SERVINGS

Chicken bones

3 large carrots

1 large onion, quartered, skin on

1 bay leaf

3 celery sticks

Handful fresh parsley

2 tsp (5 g) ground pepper

1 tsp (5 g) ground Himalayan salt

2 tbsp (19 g) garlic, minced

3 tbsp (45 ml) apple cider vinegar

Water

Optional: chicken feet or additional soup greens

To start your stock, place your bones, veggies and seasonings into the Instant Pot. Pour in your apple cider vinegar and cover with water. The amount of water will vary based on the size and quantities of your vegetables. You can also add chicken feet for extra gelatin or additional soup greens if you want. Secure the lid to your IP and press the Manual button. Then press the "+" button to increase the minute display to 90 minutes. Make sure the pressure valve on top is closed and allow your stock to cook. Once complete, quick-release the pressure valve allowing the steam to escape.

TIP: Keep your onion skins on for a darker, richer broth. Also, when freezing, consider using smaller quantities for easier thawing, such as ice cube trays and small jars.

ALTERNATIVE: If making in a slow cooker, follow the directions above and allow the stock to cook for 24–48 hours. If your slow cooker has an automatic turn-off switch, be sure to take this into account so your stock doesn't go to waste.

BEEF STOCK

Just like homemade chicken stock, homemade beef stock is so easy and cost effective, you'll wonder why you didn't start doing this long ago! You can reuse the bones more than once, so be sure not to toss them after your first batch. And don't leave out the apple cider vinegar; it helps draw the minerals out of the bones!

MAKES: 10 SERVINGS

2 lb (907 g) beef soup bones

3 large carrots

1 large onion, quartered, skin on

1 bay leaf

3 celery sticks

Handful fresh parsley

2 tsp (5 g) ground pepper

1 tsp (5 g) ground Himalayan salt

2 tbsp (19 g) garlic, minced

3 tbsp (45 ml) apple cider vinegar

Water

Optional: additional soup greens

Ideally, baking the bones at 375°F (190°C) for 30 minutes prior to pressure cooking them helps draw out the marrow, but if you only have access to your pressure cooker, it will still get the job done. To start your stock, place your bones, veggies and seasonings into the Instant Pot. Pour in your apple cider vinegar and cover with water. The amount of water will vary based on the size and quantities of your vegetables. You can add in extra greens if you want. Secure the lid to your IP and press the Manual button. Then press the "+" button to increase the minute display to 90 minutes. Make sure the pressure valve on top is closed and allow your stock to cook. Once complete, quick-release the pressure valve, allowing the steam to escape.

TIPS: Keep your onion skins on for a darker, richer stock. Also, when freezing, consider freezing in smaller quantities for easier thawing like ice cube trays and small jars.

ALTERNATIVE: If making in a slow cooker, follow the directions above and allow the stock to cook for 24–48 hours on the highest setting. If your slow cooker has an automatic turn-off switch, be sure to take this into account so your stock doesn't go to waste.

CREAM OF MUSHROOM SOUP

This soup is a great base to make dishes like green bean casserole or is perfect eaten alone as I often enjoy it. You'll be shocked at how much better homemade cream of mushroom soup tastes compared to the canned stuff. And as easy as it is to make, why would anyone want anything but homemade?!

MAKES: 6 SERVINGS

2 tbsp (30 ml) avocado oil, olive oil, ghee or preferred cooking fat

1 onion, diced

1 lb (450 g) white mushrooms, chopped

4 cups (946 ml) Beef Stock (page 82) or organic store-bought

1 tbsp (2 g) herbs de Provence

½ tsp sea salt

1 tsp (2 g) ground black pepper

1 tsp (1 g) dried parsley

½ cup (118 ml) coconut milk (or preferred dairy-free milk)

1–2 tbsp (6–12 g) arrowroot, tapioca or cassava flour

Begin by pressing the Sauté button on your Instant Pot and heat the oil for a minute. Then cook your onions and mushrooms, shifting them regularly, for about 5–8 minutes until they soften. Add in the remaining ingredients except for the coconut milk and arrowroot, give it a quick stir and secure the lid. Close the pressure valve and press the Soup button (high pressure, 30 minutes). Allow the soup to cook. Quick-release the pressure valve once finished, removing the lid once safe to do so. Use an immersion blender to purée the contents or, if desired, transfer the soup to a traditional blender and blend until pureed. Now make a slurry with the coconut milk and arrowroot by whisking them together, pour the slurry into the soup and stir once more until it begins to thicken. Serve right away as soup, or if using in a casserole, add an additional few tablespoons (12–18 g) of arrowroot slurry to thicken further.

ALTERNATIVE: If using a slow cooker, you'll need to sauté the onions and mushrooms in a skillet prior to transferring them to the slow cooker basin. Then add in the remaining ingredients except for the milk and arrowroot. Cook on low for 2–3 hours or high for about an hour, and then purée and follow remaining instructions above.

SAVORY LAMB GOULASH

This family friendly dish is also great for entertaining. It's a great switch from your typical beef and chicken dinners by packing in lots of savory veggies and the delicious smokiness of cumin and paprika. Topping it with cilantro makes it even better!

MAKES: 4 SERVINGS

1 tbsp (15 ml) avocado oil, ghee, olive oil or preferred cooking fat

1 bell pepper, seeded and diced

2 Yukon gold potatoes, diced

1 onion, diced

1 cup (150 g) carrots, chopped

1 lb (450 g) pasture-raised ground lamb or ground lamb sausage

1½ cups (240 g) fire roasted diced tomatoes or plain diced tomatoes

1 cup (240 ml) organic homemade Chicken Stock (page 81) or high-quality store-bought

1 tsp (2 g) garlic powder

1 tsp (2 g) cumin

1 tsp (2 g) paprika

1 tsp (2 g) smoked paprika

1 tsp (2 g) onion powder

½ tsp sea salt

½ tsp ground black pepper

To serve: Fresh cilantro and dairy-free sour cream

Place your cooking fat, bell pepper, potatoes, onion, carrots and ground lamb into the stainless steel basin of the Instant Pot. Press the Sauté button and cook the contents for about 5 minutes, breaking up the lamb into crumbles as it cooks. Add in the remaining ingredients except for the cilantro and sour cream and secure the lid. Now close the pressure valve and press the Meat/Stew button (high pressure, 35 minutes), and then reduce the time to 10 minutes by pressing the "-" button until the display reads accordingly.

Allow the stew to cook. Quick-release the pressure valve once complete. Remove the lid once safe to do so, press the Keep Warm/Cancel button and then the Sauté button. Sauté for 5 additional minutes to help reduce any excess liquid and create a thicker goulash. Serve with fresh cilantro and dairy-free sour cream if desired.

ALTERNATIVE: If using a slow cooker, you'll want to cook the lamb in a skillet over high heat for around 5 minutes, crumbling it as it cooks. Transfer it to your slow cooker and add in the remaining ingredients. Stir to combine, and then cook on low for 4–6 hours or 2–3 on high.

LOADED BAKED POTATO SOUP

One of my favorite soups before going grain-free and dairy-free was loaded baked potato soup with heavy cream, lots of cheese, chives and bacon. Aside from the dairy, many potato soups are thickened with flour, which is extraneous, as the potatoes themselves supply enough starch to make a thick, rich soup. This version is free of both dairy and grain yet holds on to that creamy heartiness of the original.

MAKES: 10 SERVINGS

1 tbsp (15 ml) cooking fat (ghee, avocado oil, olive oil)

1 onion, chopped

6 medium/large Yukon gold or 6 small russet potatoes

32 oz (907 ml) Chicken Stock (page 81)

1–2 tsp (5-10 g) sea salt (or to taste)

½ tsp celery salt

1 tsp (2 g) onion powder

½ tsp black pepper

1 tsp (2 g) garlic powder (or 3 cloves fresh garlic)

1 cup (240 ml) almond milk, coconut milk or preferred dairy-free milk

Toppings: 8 oz (227 g) crisped bacon, freshly minced chives and dairy-free cheese

Plug in your Instant Pot and press the Sauté feature. Drizzle in the cooking fat and toss in the onion. Sauté until the onion is translucent, or about 8 minutes. Then add in your potatoes, stock and seasonings, reserving only the milk and garnishes for later. Secure the lid and close the pressure valve. Now press the Soup button (high pressure, 30 minutes) and allow the contents to cook. Once complete, quick-release the pressure valve and remove the lid once safe to do so. Now use an immersion blender to purée the contents until smooth. Pour in the dairy-free milk and stir to combine. Add any additional salt or pepper as desired. Serve at once topped with bacon, chives and dairy-free cheese (or grass-fed organic if tolerated).

ALTERNATIVE: If using a slow cooker, place all of the ingredients in the basin except for the milk and garnishes. Cook on low for 6 hours, and then use an immersion blender to purée until there are no more chunks of potato. Add the milk, stir and allow to cook for 30 more minutes on high or until heated through. If it is not thick enough, you can make a slurry by taking ¼ cup (60 ml) of the soup and stirring in 2–3 tablespoons (12–18 g) of tapioca starch, then reintroduce it into the slow cooker, stirring to combine until it's reached desired consistency.

COWBOY CHILI

When the weather turns cooler, there is nothing I like better than a big bowl of hearty chili. You'll never miss the beans with this "stick to your ribs" recipe where I blend grass-fed ground beef and sausage for a savory celebration!

MAKES: 8 SERVINGS

1 lb (450 g) pasture-raised breakfast sausage

1 lb (450 g) grass-fed ground beef

2 onions, diced

29 oz (822 g) diced tomatoes

1 ½ cups (300 g) carrots, diced

½ tsp pepper

2 tbsp (14 g) chili powder

1 tsp (2 g) garlic powder

1 tsp (2 g) onion powder

½ tsp paprika (regular or smoked)

1 tsp (5 g) sea salt

1 tbsp (15 ml) (or more) gluten-free Worcestershire sauce

To serve: Dairy-free sour cream, jalapeño slices and dairy-free cheese

Begin by placing your two meats and onion into the basin. Press the Sauté button and cook until the meats are no longer pink, shifting the contents regularly to break them up. This will take around 5 minutes or so. Now add in the remaining ingredients. Give them a quick stir and press the Keep Warm/Cancel button (high pressure, 30 minutes). Now secure the lid, close off the pressure valve and press the Bean/Chili button. Allow the contents to cook and once complete, quick-release the pressure valve. Remove the lid when safe to do so and press Keep Warm/Cancel, and then press the Sauté button. This will help reduce the chili liquid and help thicken it up. Sauté your chili for about 10 minutes, stirring each minute or so. Serve with dairy-free sour cream, jalapeño slices and dairy-free cheese.

ALTERNATIVE: To make in a slow cooker, first sauté the breakfast sausage, beef and onions over high heat for about 5 minutes. Transfer to slow cooker and combine remaining ingredients. Give it a quick stir, cover and cook on low for 5 hours.

CREAMY TOMATO SOUP

From high school on, I used to frequent a restaurant with the BEST creamy tomato soup. With heavy cream and all the right seasonings, it always hit the spot when I was craving comfort foods. I've re-created that comfort right in the convenience of the Instant Pot and added in extra veggies for nutrients and flavor!

MAKES: 10 SERVINGS

29 oz (822 g) freshly diced tomatoes (or 2 cans)

1 large sweet potato, coarsely chopped

½ cup (75 g) chopped carrots

2 onions, coarsely chopped

1 tbsp (9 g) minced garlic

4 cups (946 ml) Chicken Stock (page 81) or organic store-bought

2 tbsp (30 ml) avocado oil, ghee or olive oil

2 tsp (10 g) sea salt

2 tsp (5 g) ground black pepper

1 tsp (1 g) dried basil (or fresh to taste)

¼ cup (60 ml) full-fat coconut milk

2 tbsp (12 g) arrowroot

Optional: fresh basil to garnish

Combine all of the ingredients, minus the coconut milk, arrowroot and basil in the Instant Pot. Secure the lid and close the pressure valve. Press the Soup button, which should display a 30-minute reading. Allow it to cycle and then quick-release the pressure valve. Once you are able, remove the lid and purée the contents. Now make a slurry with the coconut milk and arrowroot by stirring the two and add the slurry to the soup. Stir once more and serve with fresh basil to garnish.

BUTTERNUT SQUASH BISQUE

Always a fall favorite, this soup can really be made any time of year by utilizing some of your homemade Chicken Stock (page 81). Many stores now have the option to buy your butternut squash pre-diced, which makes it that much easier!

MAKES: 8 SERVINGS

32 oz (907 g) butternut squash, chopped

1 medium sweet potato, peeled and chopped

1 large onion, chopped

2 tbsp (30 ml) ghee, olive oil, avocado oil or coconut oil

1 tsp (2 g) onion powder

½ tsp paprika

1 tsp (3 g) minced garlic

1 tsp (5 g) sea salt

½ tsp ground black pepper

32 oz (907 ml) Chicken Stock (page 81)

Optional: ½ cup (118 ml) coconut milk

To begin, sauté your squash, sweet potato and onion in the cooking oil in the bottom of your pressure cooker for 5 minutes. Once complete, add the remaining ingredients, except for the milk, secure the lid and press the Soup button. Allow the soup to cook and then quick-release the steam and carefully remove the lid. Add in the coconut milk at this time. Now you may use either an immersion blender or a traditional blender to purée the ingredients until creamy.

ITALIAN WEDDING SOUP

This soup is a favorite for many and can bring back a flood of memories as well. With my pressure-cooked version, you'll quickly bring together savory turkey meatballs with a rich broth of onion, carrots and spinach.

MAKES: 8 SERVINGS

FOR THE MEATBALLS

1 lb (450 g) organic ground turkey

3 tbsp (18 g) cassava flour, tapioca, arrowroot or almond flour

3 tbsp (45 ml) coconut milk

2 tbsp (30 ml) coconut aminos

1 tbsp (15 ml) 100% maple syrup

1 tsp (2 g) garlic powder

Pinch sea salt

Optional: 1 tbsp (6 g) nutritional yeast

1 tbsp (15 ml) avocado oil, ghee or lard

FOR THE SOUP

1 onion, diced

64 oz (2 L) organic or homemade stock (I used half Beef Stock [page 82]/ half Chicken Stock [page 81])

1 cup (200 g) carrots, diced

½ tsp onion powder

½ tsp garlic powder

½ tsp sea salt

Pepper to taste

1 cup (30 g) spinach, chopped

Optional: 1 cup (165 g) grain-free, gluten-free couscous (this is sold in the Jewish foods section or can be ordered online)

Optional: 1–2 tbsp (6-12 g) tapioca, arrowroot or cassava flour

Preheat your oven to 350°F (175°C) in order to make the meatballs. If you do not have an oven, you have the option to cook them in your Instant Pot. Meanwhile, assemble your meatballs by combining meatball ingredients, except for the cooking fat, in a bowl and mix well by hand. Form meatballs between 1 and 2 inches (3 and 6 cm) in diameter and place on a parchment-lined baking sheet. Bake for 10–12 minutes and then remove from oven. If using the IP method to cook your meatballs, press the Sauté button and drizzle the cooking fat into the stainless steel bowl of your Instant Pot. Place the assembled meatballs into the bowl and brown them on all sides until they are firmly intact, or about 5 minutes. They do not need to be cooked entirely through as they will continue cooking in the broth. Now continue using the sauté feature to cook your diced onion until it is slightly translucent and begins to brown. If you need to add a bit of additional cooking fat, you can do that now.

Next, add in your stock, meatballs, carrots and seasonings, reserving the spinach for later. If you are using grain-free couscous, you can add that now as well. Now secure the lid of your Instant Pot, close the pressure valve and press the Soup button (high pressure, 30 minutes). Allow the cooking cycle to complete, and then you can quick-release your steam valve. Once it is safe to open, you can remove the lid and toss in your chopped spinach. Stir well until spinach wilts.

At this time, if you want to thicken your soup and did not use the grain-free couscous (which naturally thickens it), you can make a slurry with tapioca, arrowroot or cassava flour. To do this, remove ¼ cup (60 ml) of the broth and whisk in the starch until it has dissolved. Now add the slurry back into the soup pot, stirring until it thickens, usually a couple of minutes.

SOUTHERN SHRIMP CHOWDER

While you won't find corn or heavy cream in this chowder, it is hearty and satisfying with cauliflower rice, red pepper, onions, coconut milk and a bit of Cajun seasoning. You'll love this healthier version and feel just as satisfied as you did with the traditional one!

MAKES: 4 SERVINGS

2 tbsp (30 ml) ghee

2 ribs celery, minced

1 large onion, diced

1 red pepper, diced

1 cup (230 g) cauliflower, riced

8 oz (227 ml) Chicken Stock (page 81)

1 (15-oz [425-ml]) can coconut milk

1 heaping tsp (2 g) Cajun seasoning

½ tsp garlic powder

½ tsp onion powder

2 cups (650 g) raw frozen shrimp

3 tbsp (18 g) arrowroot, tapioca or cassava flour

Additional sea salt and pepper, to taste

Combine the ghee, celery, onion and red pepper in the stainless steel bowl of your Instant Pot. Press the Sauté button and cook for 5 minutes, or until the vegetables begin to soften. Now press the Keep Warm/Cancel button. Add the remaining ingredients except for the arrowroot and give them a quick stir. Secure the lid and close the pressure valve. Now press the Soup button, and then the "-" button until 10 minutes is displayed. Allow the cooking cycle to complete, and then quick-release the pressure valve, removing the lid when safe to do so. Now remove ½ cup (118 ml) of the broth and whisk in your 3 tablespoons (18 g) of arrowroot or preferred starch. Once it is fully incorporated, stir the slurry back into the main pot, allowing the chowder to thicken; this will take just a minute or so while stirring. Now add your sea salt and pepper to taste.

ALTERNATIVE: If using a slow cooker, combine all of the ingredients in the slow cooker except for the arrowroot starch. Allow the mixture to cook on low for 4 hours. Now remove ½ cup (118 ml) of the stock and whisk in your 3 tablespoons (18 g) of arrowroot or preferred starch. Once it is fully incorporated, stir the slurry back into the main pot, allowing the chowder to thicken; this will take just a minute or so while stirring.

VEGETABLE BEEF SOUP

This is another classic example of how to stretch your dollar and pack in extra nutrients at the same time. This recipe includes nine different vegetables in one dish and is just as perfect for chilly nights as it is for warmer ones!

MAKES: 10 SERVINGS

1 lb (450 g) grass-fed beef

32 oz (907 ml) Beef Stock (page 82)

1 large onion, diced

1 zucchini squash, diced

1 yellow squash, diced

1 cup (150 g) carrots, chopped

1 sweet potato, diced

8 oz (227 g) button mushrooms, chopped

1 red bell pepper

1 yellow bell pepper

1 cup (200 g) green beans, diced

2 tsp (10 g) sea salt or more to taste

1 tsp (2 g) ground black pepper

1 tsp (2 g) onion powder

1 tsp (2 g) paprika

1 tsp (2 g) garlic powder

1 bay leaf

Begin by browning the ground beef on the Sauté feature for about 5–7 minutes. The beef need not be perfectly cooked through since it will be heated with the soup during the pressure cooking. Now add in your stock, vegetables and seasonings and give the mixture a quick stir. Next secure the lid and close off the pressure valve. Press the Soup button (30 minutes will be displayed) and allow the cooking cycle to complete. Quick-release the pressure valve and remove the lid when safe to do so. Remove the bay leaf and serve warm.

ALTERNATIVE: If making in a slow cooker, cook the beef in a skillet over high heat for about 8 minutes. Transfer the beef to a slow cooker and add in the remaining ingredients, giving them a quick stir. Now allow the mixture to cook for 5 hours on low.

EGG ROLL SOUP

Ever have an immense craving for egg rolls and need them almost instantly? Well this recipe was born from such a craving. No need to fry with this one, just cook the meat, mix in the veggies and the work is basically done! Egg roll craving satisfied and much healthier at that!

MAKES: 6 SERVINGS

1 lb (450 g) ground pastured pork

1 tbsp (15 ml) ghee, avocado oil or olive oil

1 large onion, diced

32 oz (4 cups [946 ml]) Chicken Stock (page 81) or Beef Stock (page 82)

½ head cabbage, chopped

2 cups (680 g) shredded carrots

1 tsp (2 g) garlic powder

1 tsp (2 g) onion powder

1 tsp (5 g) sea salt

1 tsp (2 g) ground ginger

⅔ cup (158 ml) coconut aminos

Optional: 2-3 tbsp (19-28 g) tapioca starch

In your Instant Pot, brown the ground pork in the tablespoon (15 ml) of cooking fat with the diced onion, and cook until it is no longer pink. Add in the remaining ingredients, except for the tapioca, close the lid and seal the pressure valve. Now press the Keep Warm/Cancel button, then press the Soup button (high pressure, 30 minutes) and allow to cook. Quick-release the pressure valve upon completion, then remove the lid when safe to do so. If you want a thicker soup, remove ¼ cup (60 ml) of broth from the soup and stir in 2-3 tablespoons (19-28 g) of tapioca starch. Reintroduce the slurry and stir well; it will thicken over the next few minutes.

ALTERNATIVE: If making in a slow cooker, brown the ground pork in the tablespoon (15 ml) of cooking fat over high heat in a skillet for about 8 minutes. Transfer the meat to your slow cooker and add the remaining ingredients except for the tapioca starch. Cook your soup on low for 5 hours. If you would like to thicken it, remove ¼ cup (60 ml) of the broth and whisk in 2-3 tablespoons (19-28 g) of tapioca starch. Reintroduce the slurry into the soup and stir to thicken.

FISH CURRY (GREEN)

The very thought of pressure-cooked fish can sound quite scary, for fear of overcooking or compromising the texture. But if done correctly, it can be a perfect way to achieve tender fish, such as with this light, yet savory, green curry. It is mild in flavor but delicious and filling when served with cauliflower rice or over zucchini noodles.

MAKES: 2 SERVINGS

1 tbsp (15 ml) avocado oil, olive oil or preferred cooking fat

1 large onion, diced

2 cloves garlic, minced

8 oz (227 ml) Chicken Stock (page 81)

1 lb (450 g) wild-caught white fish (like cod, bass, haddock)

1 (15-oz [425-ml]) can full-fat coconut milk

2 tbsp (30 ml) green curry paste

1 cup (40 g) fresh cilantro

1 tsp (5 g) sea salt or more to taste

½ tsp onion powder

Optional: 1–2 tbsp (6-12 g) arrowroot powder

Additional fresh cilantro to garnish

Start by pressing the Sauté button and drizzling your cooking fat into the stainless steel bowl of your Instant Pot. Add in the onion and garlic and sauté just until softened and translucent, around 4–5 minutes. Now add in the remaining ingredients, except for the arrowroot, and press the Keep Warm/Cancel button. Stir the ingredients and secure the lid; close off the pressure valve and press the Soup button. Now press the "-" button until 10 minutes is displayed. Allow the cooking cycle to complete, and then quick-release the pressure valve. Remove the lid when safe to do so and either serve as is (if you prefer a thinner broth), or thicken with the arrowroot. If you choose to thicken your curry, remove ¼ cup (60 ml) of the broth and stir in 1–2 tablespoons (6-12 g) of arrowroot to create a slurry. Whisk the slurry until well combined; reintroduce it back to the pot. Stir the curry, allowing it to thicken over the next minute or two. Serve with fresh cilantro to garnish.

ALTERNATIVE: To slow cook, add all of the ingredients except for the arrowroot into a slow cooker basin and cook on low for 5 hours. If you wish to thicken, follow the directions above to create a slurry with the arrowroot flour. Serve with fresh cilantro to garnish.

SIMPLE BEEF STEW

This very simple beef stew recipe has received repeated praise both in my own home and by others who have made it. Sometimes it just takes the perfect combination of high quality meats, veggies and broth to make a memorable meal, regardless of its simplicity. Keep this in your rotation for a one-pot meal that can feed you through the week!

MAKES: 6 SERVINGS

1 tbsp (15 ml) avocado oil, ghee or lard

16 oz (450 g) beef tenderloin, cut (or stew meat)

1 onion, chopped

1 zucchini, chopped

3 Yukon gold potatoes, chopped

1 cup (150 g) chopped carrots

Optional: sweet potato, parsnip, turnips

2 cups (473 ml) Beef Stock (page 82)

1–2 tsp (5–10 g) sea salt (or more to taste)

1 bay leaf

1 tsp (2 g) pepper

1 tsp (2 g) paprika

1 tsp (2 g) garlic powder

1 tsp (2 g) onion powder

1 tbsp (15 ml) tomato paste

Gluten-free Worcestershire sauce to taste

2 tbsp (12 g) arrowroot flour

Turn on your Instant Pot and press Sauté; put in your oil and tenderloin. Sauté until the meat is no longer pink, and then toss in your remaining veggies. Stir to combine, and then add in the stock and seasonings except for the arrowroot. Stir once more, place the lid on your Instant Pot, secure the pressure valve and press Stew/Meat. The setting should automatically set itself for 35 minutes on high pressure. Once cooking is complete, your Instant Pot should automatically switch over to warm. You can leave it as is or quick-release the pressure. (I let mine rest and release the pressure on its own slowly.) After about 20 minutes on the Warm setting, you can open the top. Carefully ladle out about ¼ of the liquid and combine that in a small bowl with the arrowroot flour. Add the slurry back into the pot and stir to thicken. At this time you may taste the stew and see if you'd like to add additional salt; it is better to start low and add than to over-salt from the beginning. At this time you may serve the stew or leave it on the Warm setting until ready to enjoy. Remove the bay leaf before serving.

ALTERNATIVE: Place all of the ingredients into a slow cooker, reserving the arrowroot flour for later. Turn on Low for 8 hours, and then ladle out about ¼ of the liquid and combine that in a small bowl with the arrowroot flour. Add the slurry back into the pot and stir to thicken. Remove the bay leaf before serving.

CAULIFREDO SAUCE

Rich, creamy Alfredo sauce is a great alternative to tomato-based sauces but most are made with mountains of dairy and some use flour to thicken them. My version, made quickly in the Instant Pot, is comforting and creamy and is completely free of flour, using only the cauliflower to thicken! So while you may feel guilty eating it, you can quickly be reminded it is veggie based!

MAKES: 6 SERVINGS

1 head organic cauliflower, leaves removed and chopped

8 oz (227 ml) homemade Chicken Stock (page 81) or organic store-bought

2 tsp (6 g) minced garlic

½ cup (118 ml) dairy-free milk

2 tbsp (30 ml) ghee or preferred cooking fat

2 tbsp (12 g) nutritional yeast

1 tsp (5 g) sea salt

½ tsp pepper

Optional: pinch nutmeg

To serve: Grain-free pasta or Quick Zucchini Noodles (page 140)

Combine all of the ingredients in the stainless steel basin of the Instant Pot. Secure the lid and close off the pressure valve. Press the Steam button (high pressure, 10 minutes) and allow the ingredients to cook for the entire cycle. Once finished, quick-release the pressure valve and remove the lid when safe to do so. Now use an immersion blender to purée the mixture or carefully transfer the contents to a traditional blender and blend on high until puréed. Serve with grain-free pasta or my Quick Zucchini Noodles.

ALTERNATIVE: To make this in a slow cooker, combine all of the ingredients except for the milk and heat on low for 5 hours or high for 2 hours. Now add the milk and purée with either an immersion blender or in an upright blender. Serve with the aforementioned suggestions.

MUSHROOM PASTA SAUCE

Remember grandma's sauce that simmered on the stovetop all day long? While it was beyond delicious and conjures up precious memories, most of us don't have that kind of time. This Mushroom Pasta Sauce needs very little prep time and uses fresh tomatoes. So grab your Instant Pot and let's go!

MAKES: 8 SERVINGS

¼ cup (60 ml) olive oil

8 oz (227 g) button mushrooms, washed and chopped

1 large onion, chopped

5 large tomatoes, coarsely chopped

1 cup (160 g) grape tomatoes

1 tbsp (15 g) sea salt

1 tsp (2 g) black pepper

1 tsp (1 g) dried basil (or fresh to taste)

1 bay leaf

½ cup (118 ml) red wine

1 tbsp (15 ml) (or more) tomato paste

1 tbsp (9 g) minced garlic

1 tsp (2 g) paprika

½ tsp thyme

1 tsp (2 g) garlic powder

½ tsp oregano

To serve: Quick Zucchini Noodles (page 140) and Easy Grain-Free Meatballs (page 35)

Turn on your Instant Pot and press the Sauté button. Drizzle your olive oil in the basin and add the mushrooms and onion. Sauté them for 5 minutes, and then add in the remaining ingredients. Press the Keep Warm/Cancel button. Secure the lid and close the pressure valve. Select the Soup setting (high pressure, 30 minutes), allow the IP to come to pressure and cook. Once complete, quick-release the pressure valve and remove the lid once safe. Remove the bay leaf. Use an immersion blender to reach your desired consistency; it may be left chunkier if preferred or made more into a purée.

Serve over my Quick Zucchini Noodles and with my Easy Grain-Free Meatballs if desired.

ALTERNATIVE: Place all of the ingredients in the slow cooker and cook on low for 6 hours or on high for 3 hours. Remove the bay leaf. Use an immersion blender to purée or use an upright blender. Serve with the aforementioned recommendations.

BOLOGNESE

Oh man is this sauce good. It tastes like it has been simmering for hours, made with a touch of magic and, of course, lots of love. I love the touch that the bay leaf gives and also the wine and coconut milk. This unlikely combination cuts the acidity of the tomatoes and leaves you with a perfect pasta sauce.

MAKES: 4 SERVINGS

1 lb (450 g) grass-fed ground beef

1 tbsp (15 ml) ghee

1 large onion, diced

1 cup (150 g) carrots, chopped

1–2 tsp (5–10 g) sea salt

½ tsp ground black pepper

1 cup (240 ml) full-fat coconut milk

1 cup (240 ml) white wine

2 cups (473 ml) plum tomatoes, crushed

1 bay leaf

To serve: Quick Zucchini Noodles (page 140), or sweet potato starch noodles

Begin by pressing the Sauté button and browning the ground beef. After about 4 minutes, add in the diced onion, ghee and carrots and cook them on the Sauté setting as well for about 3 more minutes. Now add in the remaining ingredients and secure the lid. Press the Keep Warm/Cancel button and close off the pressure valve. Next press the Soup button and allow the Bolognese to cook for 30 minutes (on high pressure). When the cooking cycle is complete, quick-release the pressure valve and remove the lid when safe to do so. Now press the Keep Warm/Cancel button again, and then the Sauté button. Give the sauce a quick stir and allow it to sauté for another 10 minutes. You'll likely need to rest the lid on top to prevent splattering, but it is not necessary to secure the lid. Remove the bay leaf. Stir again and serve over Quick Zucchini Noodles (page 140) or sweet potato starch noodles (which can be found at Asian markets).

ALTERNATIVE: If making this in a slow cooker, brown your ground beef and ghee in a skillet on the stovetop over high heat for about 4 minutes, and then add in the carrots and onions for another 3 minutes. Now transfer the meat and remaining ingredients into a slow cooker and cook on low for 5 hours. Remove the bay leaf before serving.

BBQ SAUCE

A slowly simmered BBQ sauce is authentic as it gets, but with this pressure-cooked shortcut, nobody will know your little secret. This tomato-based, smoky sauce is sweetened only with 100 percent maple syrup too, so rest assured it is the best quality in addition to the fastest prep!

MAKES: 10 SERVINGS

1 cup (240 ml) high-quality store-bought ketchup

1 cup (240 ml) crushed organic tomatoes

½ cup (100 g) onion, diced

½ cup (118 ml) 100% maple syrup

1 tsp (2 g) onion powder

1 tsp (2 g) garlic powder

1 tsp (2 g) ground black pepper

2 tsp (10 ml) liquid smoke

Combine all of the ingredients in the stainless steel bowl of your Instant Pot. Give them a quick stir before securing the lid and closing off the pressure valve. Now press the Manual button, and then the "-" button until 5 minutes is displayed. Allow the cooking cycle to complete, and then quick-release the pressure valve and remove the lid. Next, you'll want to blend your BBQ sauce to make it smooth in texture; you can do this with an immersion blender or in a traditional blender. It should take only a minute or less to accomplish this. Store in an airtight glass container in the refrigerator.

ALTERNATIVE: Combine all of the ingredients in a slow cooker and cook on low for 6 hours or high for 3 hours. Purée using an immersion blender or an upright blender and serve warm or chill for later.

QUICK SIDES

Side dishes often take a backseat to the main event, which can mean that we fall short in eating enough micronutrient-packed veggies. Using a pressure cooker to make vegetable sides means you can save time and get the good stuff onto your plate without skimping.

In this chapter you'll find everything from Garlic Dill Carrots (page 119) to Smoky Mushrooms + Onions (page 120). Plus I'll show you how to make Potato Salad (page 131) and Picnic Perfect Egg Salad (page 128) in a fraction of the time, so even if you're running late, you'll still be the hit at your party!

GARLIC DILL CARROTS

The hardest part about making this recipe is not eating them all yourself! Unless you are cooking for one—then you are in luck. These 10-minute carrots combine garlic, ghee and fresh dill for a rather addictive combination.

MAKES: 3 SERVINGS

3 cups (450 g) chopped carrots
1 tbsp (15 ml) brown butter ghee, melted (or avocado oil, regular ghee, olive oil)
½ tsp (or more) garlic sea salt
1 tbsp (4 g) fresh dill, minced

Place all of your ingredients in the stainless steel bowl of your Instant Pot. Secure the lid and close off the pressure valve and press the Steam button. The display will read 10 minutes and it will begin cooking. Once complete, quick-release the pressure valve and remove the lid when safe to do so. Serve right away with additional fresh dill if desired.

NOTE: This recipe will create tender cooked carrots, but if you prefer more of an al dente presentation, please decrease cooking time.

ALTERNATIVE: To make in a slow cooker, place all of the ingredients in a slow cooker and cook on high for 2–3 hours or low for 4–5 hours.

SMOKY MUSHROOMS + ONIONS

This quick medley is a perfect side dish or entrée topper. It combines mushrooms and onions seasoned with smoked paprika for a savory addition to any meal. This side is great added into a creamy soup as well!

MAKES: 3 SERVINGS

1 tbsp (15 ml) ghee
1 (8-oz [227-g]) carton button mushrooms, sliced
1 onion, diced
½ tsp sea salt
2 tbsp (30 ml) coconut aminos
⅛ tsp (or more) smoked paprika

Start by melting the ghee in the stainless steel bowl of your Instant Pot by pressing the Sauté feature. Add the mushrooms, onion and seasonings and allow them to sauté for about 5 minutes. Now secure the lid and close off the pressure valve. Press the Keep Warm/Cancel button, and then press the Manual button. Now select the "-" button until the display reads 2 minutes. Once the cooking cycle completes, quick-release the pressure valve and remove the lid once safe to do so. Serve warm.

"ROASTED" RAINBOW FINGERLING POTATOES

Roasted potatoes are delicious but can typically take quite a lot of time and can certainly heat up an entire kitchen running the oven that long. These bring flavor, color and efficiency to your meal. Drizzle with a little extra ghee for even more deliciousness!

MAKES: 4 SERVINGS

½ cup (100 g) diced onion

2 tbsp (30 ml) ghee

1 tbsp (15 ml) olive oil

2 lb (907 g) rainbow fingerling potatoes

Up to 1 tsp (5 g) sea salt

¼ tsp black pepper

½ tsp onion powder

½ tsp paprika

Begin by sautéing the onion in your pressure cooker in the ghee and olive oil for 5 minutes. Add in the potatoes and seasonings and secure the lid. Press the Manual button and then the "-" button until the display reads 20 minutes. Quick-release the pressure valve when complete and carefully remove the lid. Serve warm.

ALTERNATIVE: In a slow cooker, put in all of the ingredients and turn on low for 4 hours.

ARTICHOKES WITH MELTED GHEE

Artichokes can be intimidating indeed, but they certainly don't have to be! With this method, there is very little prep work, leaving the Instant Pot to do the hard part. Served with melted grass-fed butter or ghee, make this for guests you want to impress!

MAKES: 3 SERVINGS

3 medium sized artichokes
1 cup (240 ml) water
½ lemon
Sea salt
9 tbsp (133 ml) melted ghee
(or grass-fed butter)

Start by preparing your artichokes. To do this, cut off the stems to create a flat bottom and cut an inch (3 cm) off the top of each artichoke as well. Pour your water into the IP stainless steel basin and lower in the steamer rack. Now place your artichokes on the rack, squeeze them with lemon and sprinkle a bit of sea salt on top. Secure the lid and close off the pressure valve. Press the Manual button, and then the "-" button until the display reads 22 minutes. Allow the artichokes to cook on high pressure and, when complete, quick-release the pressure valve. Once safe, remove the lid and carefully remove the artichokes from the Instant Pot. Serve with the melted ghee, divided into 3 serving bowls, each holding 3 tablespoons (45 ml).

ALTERNATIVE: If slow cooking, place about an inch (3 cm) of water in the bottom of the slow cooker, arrange the prepared artichokes and cook on high for 3–4 hours.

STIR-FRIED GARLICKY GREEN BEANS

Green beans have always been a popular veggie in our family, so I make them often.
But because they are so popular, I do like to change things up a bit and keep them interesting.
These stir-fried green beans have a twist on the typical steamed presentation with their garlic and
onion undertones. Zest a lemon peel as a garnish for an extra element of flavor.

MAKES: 4 SERVINGS

2 tbsp (30 ml) ghee, olive oil or avocado oil

1 tbsp (15 ml) olive oil

1 lb (450 g) haricots vert (thin green beans), trimmed

1–2 tbsp (10–18 g) minced garlic

½ tsp onion powder

½ tsp sea salt or more to taste

Lemon zest, optional

Begin by giving all of the ingredients except the lemon zest a 5-minute sauté before pressure cooking. This will help the garlic release the aromatics and add more intense flavor. Once you've sautéed your green beans, secure the lid, close the steam vent and press the Steam button. Now press the "-" button until the display reads 5 minutes. Allow the green beans to cook, and then quick-release the pressure valve. Once safe, remove the lid and serve right away. Garnish with fresh lemon zest if desired.

ALTERNATIVE: In a slow cooker, follow above directions and cook on low for 4 hours or high for 2 hours.

PICNIC PERFECT EGG SALAD

A good egg salad is a classic dish—be it as a main course, side dish or protein-packed snack. It can also be sort of an annoying chore and a bit time consuming. I love this method that uses the Instant Pot to boil the eggs, and then a quick run under cold water and you are just moments away from egg salad.

MAKES: 4 SERVINGS

1 cup (240 ml) water

7 pastured eggs

⅓ cup (79 ml) high-quality store-bought mayonnaise

2 tsp (10 ml) organic yellow mustard

1 tbsp (15 ml) dill relish

½ tsp onion powder

¼ tsp sea salt

¼ tsp ground black pepper

Optional: ¼ tsp dried dill

To serve: Romaine hearts and bacon crumbles

Start by pouring the water into the stainless steel basin of your Instant Pot. Lower in the steaming rack and place the eggs on top of it. Secure the lid and close off the pressure valve; select the Manual button, and then the "-" button until 8 minutes is displayed. Allow the eggs to boil and while they do, combine the remaining ingredients in a small mixing bowl.

Once the cooking cycle is complete, quick-release the pressure valve and remove the lid once safe to do so. Carefully remove the eggs and briefly run them under cold water until they are cool enough to peel. Then peel the eggs and chop them on a cutting board to desired texture. Now you can transfer them to the mixing bowl and stir the contents to combine thoroughly. I like to serve my egg salad in romaine hearts topped with bacon crumbles!

POTATO SALAD

Creamy, tangy potato salad is a great sidekick to any BBQ meal, be it brisket or ribs. My recipe uses
a blend of both mayonnaise and mustard and has a little crunch from minced celery.
Serve it alongside my BBQ Beef Short Ribs (page 60).

MAKES: 4 SERVINGS

24 oz (680 g) Yukon gold potatoes,
peeled and diced

½ cup (118 ml) water

¼ cup + 1 tbsp (75 ml) high-quality
store-bought mayonnaise

1 tbsp (15 ml) organic yellow mustard

½ sweet onion, minced

1 rib celery, minced

½ tsp celery salt

¼ tsp dried or fresh dill, minced

1 tsp (5 ml) apple cider vinegar

Pinch ground black pepper

Optional: paprika to garnish

Place the diced potatoes and water into the stainless steel bowl of your Instant Pot. Secure the lid, close the pressure valve and press the Steam button. The display should read 10 minutes (high pressure). Allow the potatoes to cook. Quick-release the pressure valve once the cycle is complete. Remove the lid once safe to do so. Drain the water from the potatoes (unless you want soupy potato salad) and stir in all the remaining ingredients. Sprinkle a bit of paprika on top to garnish.

SPAGHETTI SQUASH

Spaghetti squash has always been a great alternative to carb-heavy pastas. The drawback, however, is the time to bake them, which is often difficult on busy weeknights. With this simple method, you can have the squash "noodles" and homemade sauce ready in a flash.

MAKES: 2 SERVINGS

1 spaghetti squash

1 cup (240 ml) water

To serve: Bolognese (page 113) or Mushroom Pasta Sauce (page 110)

Slice the spaghetti squash widthwise (sliced lengthwise it will not fit in the IP). Scoop out the flesh in the center, along with the seeds. Pour the water into the basin and place the steamer rack in as well. Next place the squash fleshy-side down. You will have to stack them slightly in order to fit; this will not affect the end result. Plug in your Instant Pot and press the Manual button. Now press the "-" button until you see 9 minutes displayed. Also press the Pressure button so that Low Pressure is selected. Secure the lid and seal off the pressure valve. Allow the squash to cook. Quick-release the pressure valve, removing the lid once safe. Now use a fork to pull the "spaghetti" away from the sides of the squash. Serve with Bolognese or Mushroom Pasta Sauce.

ALTERNATIVES: If using a slow cooker, slice the squash widthwise, scoop out the flesh and seeds in the middle and place facedown. Pour in a cup (240 ml) of water and cook on low for 4 hours.

STEAMED GREENS + BACON

You don't have to be Southern to have an appreciation for collard greens, especially when they are topped with bacon! Toss in the ingredients and call 'em done!

MAKES: 4 SERVINGS

3 cups (710 ml) broth

14-16 oz (400-450 g) collard greens

3 tsp (9 g) garlic, minced

1 tsp (2 g) onion powder

½ tsp ground pepper

1 tbsp (15 ml) apple cider vinegar

8 oz (227 g) bacon, crisped and chopped

1-2 tsp (2-4 g) sea salt

Place all ingredients except for cooked bacon into the stainless steel bowl of your Instant Pot. Secure the lid, close the pressure valve and press the Steam button. Allow the cooking cycle to complete, and then quick-release the pressure valve. Remove the lid when safe to do so and use a slotted spoon or skimmer to remove the greens. Top with crisped bacon to serve and additional sea salt if needed.

ALTERNATIVE: Place all of the ingredients except for the bacon in a slow cooker. Cook on high for 3 hours, and then use a slotted spoon or skimmer to remove the greens. Top with crisped bacon and additional sea salt if needed.

PRESSURE-COOKED CRANBERRY SAUCE

I grew up on the jellied stuff out of the can and to be honest I always loved it! That is until I learned how easy it was to make homemade cranberry sauce without high fructose corn syrup! It's such a fantastic thing to make fresh for the holidays, and in the Instant Pot it's also really quick!

MAKES: 4 SERVINGS

12 oz (285 g) fresh cranberries

4 oz (113 ml) freshly squeezed orange juice

3 tbsp (45 ml) 100% maple syrup or honey

Pinch sea salt

Add all of the ingredients into the stainless steel bowl of your Instant Pot. Stir to combine them, and then secure the lid. Close the pressure valve and press the Manual button. Now press the "-" button until 2 minutes is displayed. Allow the cooking cycle to complete. Quick-release the pressure valve and remove the lid when safe to do so. Mash the cranberries and serve right away warm—or chill for later if making ahead.

"BAKED" SWEET POTATOES

Sweet potatoes are often the chosen starch among grain-free eaters. They are autoimmune friendly,
a safe starch and full of flavor to boot. Giant sweet potatoes can take ages to bake in the oven,
as delicious as they are, which makes this shortcut recipe all the more sweet . . . potato!

MAKES: 3 LARGE SERVINGS

1 cup (240 ml) water
3 extra-large sweet potatoes (I used jewel sweet potatoes)
To serve: Grass-fed butter, ghee, salsa or chili

Pour the water into the Instant Pot basin. Place the steam rack in next and stack the sweet potatoes on top of the rack. I stacked mine like a pyramid and three filled the entire pot. Secure the lid, close the pressure valve and press the Manual button. Now select the "-" button until the display reads 25 minutes. Allow the potatoes to cook, and then quick-release the pressure valve. Remove the lid when safe to do so and carefully remove the potatoes when able with a gloved hand or serving utensil. Smaller potatoes will need less time, so start on the lower end, and then add minutes if your potatoes aren't done enough. Serve topped with butter, ghee, salsa or chili.

ALTERNATIVE: To make in a slow cooker, wrap the sweet potatoes in foil and lower them into your slow cooker. Turn on the lowest setting and allow them to cook for 8 hours, or if on the high setting, 4 hours.

QUICK ZUCCHINI NOODLES

Zucchini noodles traditionally have a sort of process that goes with them: spiral cutting them, salting them, "sweating" them and then sautéing until you've reached just the right texture, without overdoing. This process cuts back on time and steps, making them even more enjoyable!

MAKES: 4 SERVINGS

4 medium-sized zucchini squash
Sea salt
½ cup (118 ml) water

Start by lining a plate with an absorbent kitchen towel or paper towel. Spiral cut your zucchini onto the towel-lined plate and salt them as they are cut (in layers between zucchini). Once they are all cut, give the zucchini noodles a quick squeeze and set aside. Now pour the water into the stainless steel bowl of your Instant Pot. Lower in a steaming basket (not the rack it comes with), and then place the zucchini noodles into the basket. Secure the lid and close the pressure valve. Press the Steam button, and then the "-" button until 5 minutes is displayed. Allow the noodles to cook. Release the valve and remove the lid once safe to do so. The noodles will be prepared with an al dente texture. If you prefer them softer, you may increase the steaming time, keeping in mind that cooking them too long will yield a mushy noodle.

HONEYED BEETS

I used to love taking those sweet pickled beets and drizzling them with ranch dressing. The cool, creamy dressing combined with the sweet, tangy beets is so satisfying. While these aren't pickled, I figured out how to create those sweet, earthy beets in just minutes, without the refined sugar or weird ingredients.

MAKES: 4 SERVINGS

4 medium red beets

1 tbsp (15 ml) walnut oil, avocado oil, olive oil or ghee

¼ cup (60 ml) local honey

2 tbsp (30 ml) 100% maple syrup

Sea salt to taste

Slice the beets as thin as you'd like using a mandoline or knife. Drizzle the cooking fat into the bottom of the stainless steel Instant Pot bowl, and then place the beets on top. Now spoon your honey and maple syrup onto the beets and secure the lid of the IP. Close off the pressure valve and press the Manual button. Now press the "-" button until 5 minutes is displayed. Allow the cooking cycle to complete, and then quick-release the pressure valve. Remove the lid when safe to do so and serve the beets warm.

You can also chill them and serve them as such on a salad. If you want to thicken the syrup and honey, remove the beets and press the Sauté button, stirring the oil, honey and syrup until it begins to thicken, just a few minutes. You may drizzle the thickened syrup over top of the beets upon serving.

ALTERNATIVE: In a slow cooker combine all of the ingredients and cook on low for 5 hours or until the beets are tender.

"CANNED" GREEN BEANS

To be honest, this recipe started as a bit of a joke, but I soon realized that there are a lot of people (including my own children) who LOVE canned green beans, even over the fresh variety. And while I personally prefer fresh green beans, canned ones still go into my grain-free green bean casserole in the fall. So I figured why not find a way to make "canned" green beans from fresh or frozen without ever opening a can! These turned out just perfect!

MAKES: 3 SERVINGS

10 oz (284 g) frozen green beans (or fresh), cut

1 tbsp (15 ml) ghee, avocado oil or olive oil

2 tbsp (30 ml) water

Pinch sea salt

Combine all of the ingredients in the stainless steel bowl of your Instant Pot. Secure the lid and close off the pressure valve. Press the Manual button, and then the "-" button until 10 minutes is displayed. Allow the green beans to cook, and then quick-release the pressure valve. Remove the lid when safe to do so and serve warm.

NOTE: If using fresh green beans, follow the above directions but reduce the time to 5 minutes instead of 10.

ALTERNATIVE: If using a slow cooker, place the green beans, water and ghee into the slow cooker and cook on low for 4 hours.

NATURALLY SWEETENED TREATS

Desserts might seem like an unlikely choice to make in your Instant Pot, but the versatility of this pressure cooker means that you can make a successful meal start to finish. Whether you are more of a brownie fan (page 161) or a pot de crème (page 158) lover, you'll find options here to fit anyone's craving. I've even included a White Chocolate Fondue (page 154) made only with the cleanest ingredients!

STRAWBERRY SHORTCAKE MUG CAKE

Mug cakes are a fun way to serve up personal-sized treats. Instead of using a microwave, these mug cakes use the Instant Pot! I made this one with fresh strawberries for a hint of sweet without being too heavy.

MAKES: 1 SERVING

1 egg

½ cup (48 g) almond flour

½ tsp 100% vanilla extract

1 tbsp (15 ml) maple syrup

1 tbsp (15 ml) ghee

3 tbsp (24 g) chopped strawberries (plus more for garnish)

1 cup (240 ml) water

3 tbsp (45 ml) coconut whipped cream to garnish

Combine all of the ingredients, except for the water and whipped cream, into a heat-resistant ceramic coffee mug. Pour the cup of water into the stainless steel Instant Pot bowl and place the wire rack into the basin. Set your mug on top of the rack and secure the lid. Seal off the pressure valve and press the Manual button. Now press the "-" button until 12 minutes is displayed. Now allow the cake to cook, quick-releasing the pressure valve when the cycle is complete. Remove the lid when safe to do so and carefully remove the hot mug. Top with coconut whipped cream and additional fresh strawberries if desired.

ALTERNATIVE: Combine all of the cake ingredients in your mug, stir and slow cook on high for 2 hours.

TAPIOCA PUDDING

Growing up, I used to love those little premade tapioca pudding cups. My grandma used to buy them for me as a treat and I'd love pulling a chilled one out of the fridge. Now when my own kids ask me for those very same pudding cups, I say "NO!" without any hesitation. The ingredient list is just not one that I can feel good about giving my kids, even with my adoration and warm childhood memories of them. So I made homemade tapioca in minutes and I feel really great about the quality and the taste! Give it a try!

MAKES: 6 SERVINGS

1 cup (240 ml) water

1 (13.5-oz [383-ml]) can coconut milk

⅓ cup (63 g) small tapioca pearls

¼ cup (60 ml) 100% maple syrup (or more)

1 tsp (5 ml) 100% vanilla extract

Pinch sea salt

Optional: ¼ tsp ground nutmeg

OPTIONAL GARNISH

Blueberries

Mint

Pour the water into the stainless steel basin and lower it into the steaming rack. Combine all of the ingredients in an oven-proof glass bowl and stir. If using the optional nutmeg, you may include that as well. This creates more of a rice pudding–type flavoring. Place the glass bowl onto the steaming rack and secure the Instant Pot lid. Secure the pressure valve closed and press the Manual button. Now press the "-" button until the display reads 20 minutes.

Allow the pudding to cook, and then quick-release the pressure valve. Once safe to do so, remove the lid. Stir the pudding vigorously as the pearls will have settled to the bottom of the glass bowl. Your pudding will not be thick yet but will thicken as it cools. Gently remove the glass bowl once it is cool enough and transfer it to the refrigerator to cool further. Stir after about 30 minutes of cooling and serve with blueberries or other fruits of your choosing. Garnish with mint if you like. Store leftovers chilled.

ALTERNATIVE: If using a slow cooker, pour the ingredients directly into the slow cooker and cook on high for 2 hours. Again, it will be soupy while still warm, but it will thicken upon cooling.

CHOCOLATE CHIP BANANA BREAD MUFFINS

Banana bread made from scratch just feels like home. This unlikely method is great if you don't want to heat the kitchen up with your oven. This recipe will yield three extra-large muffins, or you could use smaller muffin cups instead. I prefer the silicone ones for a moist muffin that pops right out!

MAKES: 3 LARGE MUFFINS

2 ripe bananas

1 egg

½ cup (118 ml) 100% maple syrup

½ cup (48 g) cassava flour

¼ cup (24 g) coconut flour

¼ cup (60 ml) preferred cooking fat (olive oil, ghee, avocado oil)

2 tsp (10 ml) 100% vanilla extract

Pinch sea salt

½ cup (80 g) dairy- and soy-free chocolate chips

½ cup (118 ml) water

Optional: pecan pieces

Blend all of the ingredients in a blender or food processor except for the chocolate chips and water. Stir in the chocolate chips and spoon the batter into your silicone muffin cups. Place the steamer rack into the basin and pour ½ cup (118 ml) water into the bottom. Rest your filled silicone muffin cups on the rack and place a piece of parchment paper gently on top of them. This will help prevent too much water dripping directly onto the muffins as they steam. Secure the lid and close the pressure valve. Now press the Manual button and the "-" button, decreasing the digital readout to 10 minutes. Allow the muffins to cook, and then quick-release the pressure valve. Remove the lid once safe to do so. Remove the muffins and sprinkle pecan pieces on top if desired. The tops may be a little wet when they first come out; remedy this by allowing them to dry out for 10–15 minutes at room temperature.

ALTERNATIVE: Follow above preparations, and then lower your muffin cups into your slow cooker and cook on high for 1 hour or until cooked through.

WHITE CHOCOLATE FONDUE

If you've ever been lucky enough to dunk fresh fruit into a white chocolate fondue, you know you felt like you were living out some sort of dream. Sweet, melted white chocolate mixed with cool fruit is so decadent despite its simplicity. I made this white chocolate fondue so that you could put on your fancy pants with literally the press of a button.

MAKES: 6 SERVINGS

2 oz (58 ml) cocoa butter

1 cup (240 ml) full-fat coconut milk

1 tsp (5 ml) 100% vanilla extract

¼ cup (60 ml) 100% maple syrup or local honey (you can use more if you prefer sweeter)

2 tbsp (19 g) tapioca starch

Combine all of the ingredients, except the tapioca starch, in the stainless steel bowl of your Instant Pot. Note: The cocoa butter will be a solid block; you need to cut it off and it will melt into more of an oil. The tapioca starch will thicken it back into a creamy dip. Secure the lid and close off the pressure valve. Press the Steam button, and then press the "-" button until 5 minutes is displayed. Allow the cooking cycle to complete. Quick-release the pressure valve and remove the lid when safe to do so. Now you want to transfer the heated mixture to a blender and give it a quick blend for 30 seconds or less. Next, in order to thicken it, you'll make a slurry. To do this, take ¼ cup (60 ml) of the mixture and whisk 2 tablespoons (19 g) of tapioca starch into it. Once combined, stir the slurry back into the main portion of the fondue. Stir for a minute or so until the fondue thickens, and serve warm with fresh fruit like strawberries or melon.

ALTERNATIVE: Combine all of the ingredients, except the tapioca starch, in your slow cooker and cook on low for 2 hours. Then follow the remaining instructions above to thicken with tapioca starch.

LEMON CUSTARD

Sometimes you need a little treat that isn't overly sweet but is light and refreshing.
This creamy lemon custard is just that and doesn't feel too heavy or rich.

MAKES: 3 SERVINGS

1 cup (240 ml) full-fat coconut cream

3 egg yolks

1 lemon, juiced

⅓ cup (79 ml) local honey or 100%
maple syrup

1 tsp (5 ml) 100% vanilla extract

1 cup (240 ml) water

Blackberries (optional)

Whisk together all of the ingredients, except the water and blackberries, in a mixing bowl. If you find that you can't get the texture smooth enough, you can transfer the mixture to a blender and give it a quick blend just until the texture is free of lumps. Now divide the custard mix into three heat-resistant glass or ceramic bowls (or cups). Pour a cup (240 ml) of water into the bottom of your stainless steel Instant Pot bowl. Lower the custard-filled cups into the bowl as well. Secure the lid and close off the pressure valve. Now press the Manual button, and then the "-" button until 10 minutes is displayed. Once the cooking cycle completes, quick-release the pressure valve and remove the lid when safe to do so. Remove the custard cups and transfer them to the refrigerator, allowing them to chill for an hour before serving. This will help them firm up. Garnish with blackberries if you desire.

CHOCOLATE POTS DE CRÈME

They may sound fancy and they might look so too, but these little creamy chocolate cups are perfect for when you need just a little something sweet. I made them in vintage glassware to make them look extra special. Add coconut whipped cream and chocolate shavings to the top and you are ready to impress just about anyone!

MAKES: 3-4 SERVINGS

1 cup (240 ml) coconut milk

3 egg yolks

½ cup (118 ml) melted dairy- and soy-free chocolate chips

2 tbsp (30 ml) maple syrup

1 cup (240 ml) water

To serve: Coconut whipped cream and dairy-free chocolate shavings

In a blender, mix together the first four ingredients until they are creamy. If you do not have a blender, make sure your eggs and coconut milk are room temperature before adding in the melted chocolate chips, or the melted chocolate will seize up and your mixture will not be creamy. Pour the chocolate mixture into appropriate glass or ceramic bowls (or cups). Now pour the water into the stainless steel bowl of your Instant Pot. Place your pots de crème into the bowl as well.

Secure the lid of your IP, close the pressure valve and press the Manual button. Now press the "-" button until 5 minutes is displayed. Allow the cooking cycle to finish. Quick-release the pressure valve and remove the lid when safe to do so. Take out your pots de crème and refrigerate them until they are cool and set, around 1 hour. Serve with coconut whipped cream and dairy-free chocolate shavings.

GRAIN-FREE BLISSFUL BROWNIES

You might wonder why anyone would want to "bake" brownies in an Instant Pot. Well, there are a few reasons honestly! Let's say you are in a college dorm with limited access to a full kitchen. Or it's summer and the heat from a conventional oven sounds like sheer torture. Or maybe due to food sensitivities you travel with your IP so you can cook on the road out of a hotel room. Whatever the case, these brownies are a great treat to pull together wherever you are!

MAKES: 6 SERVINGS

1 egg

½ cup (118 ml) cashew or almond butter

¼ cup (48 g) cassava flour (or arrowroot)

¼ tsp sea salt

¾ cup (144 g) maple sugar
(or date sugar)

⅓ cup (79 ml) 100% maple syrup

2 tbsp (30 ml) ghee or sustainable palm
shortening, melted

1 tsp (5 ml) 100% vanilla extract

3 tbsp (20 g) cocoa powder

1 cup (240 ml) water

Combine all of the ingredients, except the water, in a mixing bowl and stir to combine. Spoon the contents into a small greased glass baking dish that will fit inside your Instant Pot. Pour the water into the stainless steel bowl of your IP, and then lower it into the steaming rack. Make a foil "tent" to cover the brownies so they are protected from the moisture. Place the covered dish onto the steaming rack and secure the lid. Next, close off the pressure valve and press the Manual button. Press the "+" button until 35 minutes is displayed. Allow the brownies to cook and when the cycle is complete, quick-release the pressure valve. Remove the lid when safe to do so and carefully transfer the brownies out of the pressure cooker and into the refrigerator to set. Leave them to chill for about half an hour, and then slice and serve. You can top them with dairy- or soy-free chocolate chips or crushed nuts like pecans if you like. These are a fudgier type brownie as compared to a cakey one due to being pressure cooked.

ALTERNATIVE: Combine all of the ingredients in a mixing bowl and stir well. Spoon the batter into a greased glass baking dish and pour 1 cup (240 ml) of water into your slow cooker. Now lower in the brownies and cook covered on high for 1 ½ hours. Then cook them uncovered for another 30 minutes.

FRUIT-SWEETENED CRANBERRY ORANGE LOAVES

These little loaves are entirely fruit sweetened. I wrote them in an effort to make a treat without the added sweeteners while I was eating lower carb, so that I could still satisfy my sweet tooth without going overboard. If you prefer a sweeter treat, you could add a bit of honey or maple syrup.

MAKES: 2 MINI LOAVES

1 cup (96 g) cassava flour

½ cup (118 ml) orange juice

½ cup (118 ml) unsweetened applesauce

2 pastured eggs

1 tsp (2 g) orange zest

Pinch sea salt

½ tbsp (7 ml) apple cider vinegar

1 tsp (5 ml) pure lemon extract

1 tbsp (6 g) coconut flour

⅓ cup (50 g) fruit-sweetened dried cranberries

1 cup (240 ml) water

Dried, unsweetend cranberries, optional

Combine all of the ingredients (except for the water and unsweetened cranberries) in a mixing bowl and stir well. Spoon the batter into two mini loaf pans and cover with greased foil. Pour the water into the stainless steel bowl of your Instant Pot and lower it into the steaming rack. Place the loaf pans onto the steaming rack, secure the lid and close the pressure valve. Press the Manual button and allow the 30-minute cooking cycle to complete before quick-releasing the pressure valve and removing the lid. Carefully take out the loaf pans and allow them to cool for a few minutes before removing the loaves from the pans and serving with cranberries if you like.

ALTERNATIVE: Combine all of the ingredients (except the water) in a mixing bowl, stirring well. Now spoon batter into two greased mini loaf pans. Pour the water into the bottom of your slow cooker and lower your loaf pans into the water. Cook on high for 1 hour or until baked through.

HIDDEN SPINACH BUNDT CAKES

It's hard to believe these delicious little cakes have spinach packed into them! I used mini-Bundt pans to make the cutest veggie-packed dessert you'll ever eat, but you can use whichever shape you prefer or have on hand.

MAKES: 3-4 SERVINGS

5 eggs

2 cups (60 g) fresh organic baby spinach

¼ cup plus 1 tbsp (30 g) coconut flour

½ cup plus 1 tbsp (54 g) arrowroot flour (tapioca works too)

⅓ cup (37 g) organic cocoa powder

⅓ cup (79 ml) local raw honey or maple

1 tsp (4 g) baking soda

4 tsp (20 ml) cooking fat of choice (butter, ghee, coconut oil, olive oil)

½ tsp ground sea salt

1 tsp (5 ml) organic gluten-free vanilla

2 tbsp (24 g) coconut sugar

¼ cup (60 ml) unsweetened flax, almond or coconut milk

Optional: one handful of dairy- and soy-free chocolate chips

1 cup (240 ml) water

Place all of the ingredients into a blender except for the optional chocolate chips and water. Blend until puréed, about 1 minute. Pour the batter into greased mini-Bundt cake pans and sprinkle in chocolate chips (if using). Pour the water into the stainless steel bowl of your Instant Pot and lower in the steaming rack.

Place the filled Bundt cake pans on top of the steaming rack and cover them loosely with a piece of foil so the condensation does not interfere with the baking process. If you need to stack the pans vertically, you may do so as long as they are not resting in or on the batter beneath in the other pans.

Press the Manual button, and then the "-" button until 25 minutes is displayed. Allow the cooking cycle to complete, and then quick-release the pressure valve. Remove the lid when safe to do so and carefully remove the mini-Bundt pans when able. Gently pry the cakes out of the pans after cooling them for 5 minutes. Serve warm.

ALTERNATIVE: Combine all of the ingredients (except for the water) in a mixing bowl, stirring well. Now spoon batter into greased mini-Bundt cake pans. Pour the water into the bottom of your slow cooker and lower your loaf pans into the water. Cook on high for 1 hour or until baked through.

INDIVIDUAL CHEESECAKES WITH GRAHAM CRUST

Cheesecake in a pressure cooker made without dairy? It sounds like utter nonsense but it's not! In fact, this little treasure was so delightful I barely finished photographing it before my 5-year-old ate it off the prop table!

MAKES: 2 SERVINGS

FOR THE CRUST

½ cup (48 g) coconut flour

½ cup (60 g) pecan meal (pulse in blender or food processor from whole pecans)

¼ tsp salt

¼ tsp baking soda

1 tsp (2 g) cinnamon

¼ cup (60 ml) honey

¼ cup (60 ml) coconut oil, melted

1 egg

1 tsp (5 ml) 100% vanilla extract

FOR THE FILLING

1½ cups (195 g) raw cashews, soaked for 4 hours or more

¼ cup (60 ml) coconut oil, melted

¼ cup (60 ml) 100% maple syrup

⅓ cup (79 ml) dairy-free milk (flax, coconut, almond)

Pinch sea salt

1 cup (240 ml) water

Ground cinnamon to sprinkle over the top

Coconut whipped cream, to serve

To make the crust, combine all of the ingredients in a blender and blend until puréed. Divide into two equal amounts and spoon the crust into two individual-sized ceramic tart dishes. Place them in the freezer and prepare the filling.

To make the filling, combine all of the ingredients in a blender and blend until puréed. The filling will be slightly thinner than the crust. Remove the crusts from the freezer and spoon the filling into each of them. Pour the water into the stainless steel bowl of your Instant Pot. Lower in one tart dish and loosely cover with parchment paper. Lower in the IP steam rack and place the second tart dish on top of it, also covering it loosely with parchment paper. The paper will prevent moisture from dripping into the cheesecakes while they cook.

Now secure the lid, close off the pressure valve and press the Manual button and then the "-" button until 10 minutes is displayed. Allow the cooking cycle to complete. Then quick-release the pressure valve. Remove the lid when safe to do so and carefully transition the cheesecakes to the refrigerator to set for about an hour. To serve, sprinkle some additional cinnamon or top with coconut whipped cream.

ALTERNATIVE: To make in a slow cooker, follow preparation steps above, and then pour 1 cup (240 ml) water into your slow cooker and lower in the cheesecake-filled dishes. Cook on high for 2 hours, remove and chill for an hour before serving.

HOT BEVERAGES IN A BLINK

Hot beverages have never been easier. Rather than make you stand over a stovetop constantly stirring, these drinks come together quickly and allow you to take more time doing other things in the kitchen—or elsewhere for that matter!

Once your drinks are "cooked," the Instant Pot will automatically switch over to a warming feature. This way you can keep your selected beverage warm if serving others or entertaining. It's a great convenience, like a slow cooker, but will heat the drink of your choosing in a fraction of the time.

In this chapter, you can find warm beverages like Hands-Free Hot Chocolate (page 175), Chai Tea Lattes (page 171) and even 5-Minute Eggnog (page 179)! Whether you serve them hot right away or chill for later, you'll love how easy these drinks come together in just one pot!

CHAI TEA LATTE

A warm, perfectly spiced chai tea latte need not be $5 a pop. It also doesn't need to be made with yucky ingredients. This creamy, hot beverage is easy enough to make at home quickly and can even be made ahead and reheated!

MAKES: 3 SERVINGS

3 organic black tea bags

1 tsp (2 g) ground cinnamon

½ tsp ground ginger

¼ tsp allspice

1 cup (240 ml) water

1 (13.5-oz [372-ml]) can coconut milk

3 tbsp (45 ml) 100% maple syrup

Pinch ground cloves

Optional: coconut whipped cream

Combine all of the ingredients in the stainless steel Instant Pot bowl and give them a quick stir. Secure the lid and close off the pressure valve. Press the Steam button; the display will read 10 minutes. Allow the cooking cycle to complete. Quick-release the pressure valve and remove the lid once safe to do so. Top with coconut whipped cream if you'd like. If ingredients separate while cooking, simply use an immersian blender to make them uniform once again.

ALTERNATIVE: In a slow cooker, combine all of the ingredients and stir. Warm on low for 2–3 hours.

ORANGE POMEGRANATE TEA

I love making tea in my Instant Pot because when I am making bigger batches, I don't have to stir or keep an eye on it on the stovetop. I've had so much fun experimenting with different flavors and combinations that normally I might not try because of the "steps" to get to the final product. Now I just toss everything in and come back when it beeps at me. You can't beat it!

MAKES: 3 SERVINGS

16 oz (450 ml) water
8 oz (227 ml) 100% pomegranate juice
2 tbsp (30 ml) honey
2 black tea bags (single serving)
1 orange-flavored tea bag (single serving)

Pour the water and juice into the stainless steel Instant Pot bowl. Add the honey and stir to combine. Now toss your tea bags in and secure the lid. Close the pressure valve and press the Steam button. Now press the "-" button until 5 minutes is displayed. Allow the tea to steep, and release the pressure valve before removing the lid. Stir once more and serve right away! If serving later, remove the tea bags so they will not continue to steep.

ALTERNATIVE: If making in a slow cooker, combine all of the ingredients (as in the instructions above), and turn your slow cooker on to the lowest setting for 2-3 hours.

HANDS-FREE HOT CHOCOLATE

Kids love it; adults love it; everybody loves it! The perfect winter beverage is and will always be hot chocolate. This not-too-sweet, creamy hot cocoa is made with coconut milk for a dairy-free alternative. It's ever-so-delicious topped with coconut whipped cream or homemade marshmallows!

MAKES: 3 SERVINGS

3 cups (710 ml) coconut milk (or flax, almond, cashew milk)

1 tbsp (7 g) organic cocoa powder

2 tbsp (24 g) coconut palm sugar

2 tbsp (30 ml) 100% maple syrup

Optional: ground cinnamon to taste, ⅛ teaspoon nutmeg, coconut whipped cream or homemade marshmallows

Combine the dairy-free milk, cocoa powder, palm sugar and maple syrup in the stainless steel basin of your Instant Pot and secure the lid. Close the pressure valve and press the Manual button, and then press the "-" button until 5 minutes is displayed. Allow the hot chocolate to heat, and then quick-release the pressure valve. Remove the lid once safe to do so and stir it. Or better yet, give it a quick blend with an immersion blender. Serve warm or use the warming feature to keep it hot if you are entertaining. Add cinnamon and nutmeg and top with coconut whipped cream or marshmallows.

ALTERNATIVE: In a slow cooker, combine all of the ingredients and stir. Warm on low for 2–3 hours.

MULLED CIDER

Mulled cider is such a fun winter favorite, and it reminds me so much of the Glühwein we drank at the Christmas markets when living overseas in Germany. While this cider is made free of alcohol, it has the same warming spices and hint of citrus. Instead of slow-cooking on the stovetop, this version is made very quickly in the Instant Pot.

MAKES: 4 SERVINGS

6 cups (1.5 L) apple cider

2 cinnamon sticks

8 whole cloves

1 clementine (mandarin), sliced with peel still on

1 lemon, sliced with peel still on

Place all of your ingredients into the stainless steel bowl of the Instant Pot. Secure the lid, close off the pressure valve and press the Steam button. Now press the "+" button until the display reads 20 minutes. Allow the steam cycle to complete. Quick-release the pressure valve and remove the lid once safe to do so. Serve right away or use the Keep Warm/Cancel feature to keep your cider warm until ready to serve.

ALTERNATIVE: In a slow cooker, combine all of the ingredients and stir. Warm on low for 2–3 hours.

5-MINUTE EGGNOG

Rich, creamy eggnog is always a fun holiday treat, especially sprinkled with nutmeg. Once I realized how easy it was to make my own, I was hooked. This version is cooked for those who are squeamish about raw eggs. I've been using this recipe as coffee creamer year round, so it doesn't have to just be a winter indulgence!

MAKES: 4 SERVINGS

6 pastured eggs

1 tsp (5 ml) 100% vanilla extract

¼ cup (60 ml) 100% maple syrup

4 cups (946 ml) coconut milk

2 tsp (10 ml) ghee

¼ tsp nutmeg

To serve: Coconut whipped cream and nutmeg

Combine all of the ingredients in the stainless steel bowl of your Instant Pot. Whisk to combine them so the eggs are incorporated well. Secure the lid, close the pressure valve and press the Manual button. Now press the "-" button until 5 minutes is displayed. Allow the cooking cycle to complete. Quick-release the pressure valve and remove the lid when safe to do so.

Check your eggnog; if there are any "eggy" bits, transfer the cooked mixture to your blender and give it a quick blend. Just a few seconds is all it will take to smooth out your eggnog. Store in a covered container in the refrigerator until ready to use. Top with homemade coconut whipped cream and an extra sprinkle of nutmeg.

ALTERNATIVE: Combine all of the ingredients in your slow cooker and warm on low for 2 hours. Blend if necessary, then chill before serving.

PEPPERMINT COCOA

Without the peppermint extract, this makes a fantastic mug of traditional hot chocolate. But life is a little more exciting when you shake things up. So when the temperatures drop and you are feeling decadent, make this peppermint cocoa, top it with coconut whipped cream and a few vegetable-dyed sprinkles to make it extra special. Bottoms up!

MAKES: 3 SERVINGS

2 (14-oz [385-ml]) cans coconut milk

½ tsp pure peppermint extract

3 tbsp (45 ml) 100% maple syrup

3 tbsp (20 g) organic cocoa powder

Optional: coconut whipped cream and dye-free sprinkles

Combine the first four ingredients in the stainless steel bowl of your Instant Pot and stir to combine. The cocoa powder may not be completely dissolved into the milk; this is all right. It will incorporate more upon cooking. Secure the lid, close the pressure valve and press the Steam button. Now press the "-" button until 5 minutes is displayed. Allow the cooking cycle to complete. Quick-release the pressure valve and remove the lid when safe to do so. Use an immersion blender to give it a quick blend if your milk has separated. Ladle into mugs, top with coconut whipped cream and naturally dyed sprinkles for an extra special treat!

ALTERNATIVE: Combine all of the ingredients, except the coconut whipped cream and the spinkles, in your slow cooker and whisk. Cook on low for 2–3 hours. Blend until the hot chocolate is uniform in nature. Serve topped with coconut whipped cream and naturally dyed sprinkles, if desired.

HONEY LEMON SOOTHER

This feels like the perfect drink when you are craving lemonade in the winter!
Plus, it has soothing honey—perfect if you feel a bit of a sore throat coming on.

MAKES: 3 SERVINGS

3 cups (710 ml) water
½ cup (118 ml) lemon juice
½ tsp ground ginger
¼ cup (60 ml) honey (or more to taste)

Combine all of the ingredients in the stainless steel bowl of your Instant Pot. Secure the lid, close the pressure valve and press the Steam button. Now press the "-" button until 5 minutes is displayed. Allow the cooking cycle to complete, and then quick-release the pressure valve. Remove the lid when safe to do so and serve warm.

ALTERNATIVE: In a slow cooker, combine all of the ingredients and stir. Warm on low for 2–3 hours.

QUICK REFERENCE GUIDE
INSTANT POT FEATURES AND TIMES

- **Sauté function** – this feature is used to sauté with the IP lid off and can also be used to simmer or if you want to reduce a liquid.

- **Keep Warm/Cancel button** – this feature is used to cancel another cook feature (and keep warm) or to turn off your IP.

- **Manual button** – this feature is used when you wish to customize your cooking cycle. It will allow you to select time and then pressure level by selecting Manual first.

- **Soup** – this feature will automatically cook at high pressure for 30 minutes.

- **Meat/Stew** – this feature will automatically cook at high pressure for 35 minutes.

- **Bean/Chili** – this feature will automatically cook at high pressure for 30 minutes.

- **Poultry** – this feature will automatically cook at high pressure for 15 minutes.

- **Rice** – this feature will automatically cook at low pressure for 12 minutes. (Note: rice may not be suitable for a Paleo lifestyle.)

- **Multi-grain** – this feature automatically cooks at high pressure for 40 minutes. (Note: grains are not considered Paleo as a general rule of thumb.)

- **Porridge** – this feature automatically cooks at high pressure for 20 minutes.

- **Steam** – this feature automatically cooks at high pressure for 10 minutes.

For more information, please refer to your Instant Pot manual.

ACKNOWLEDGMENTS

To my little Robins nest, for eating pressure-cooked meals for many consecutive months. Your willingness to try new foods is always so refreshing and makes my "job" so much easier.

To my friends, who have continued to support my creative drive and who also tell me when it's time to practice more self-care.

To Page Street Publishing, for my fourth opportunity to publish—two years ago I knew nothing about writing books, and now I've been able to accomplish authorship four times over.

ABOUT THE AUTHOR

Jennifer Robins is the voice and whole-foodist behind the popular food blog Predominantly Paleo, and bestselling author of *Down South Paleo*, *The New Yiddish Kitchen* and *Paleo Kids Cookbook*. After being diagnosed with several autoimmune conditions and chronic infections, including Lyme disease, Jennifer became gravely ill and mostly housebound. When traditional medical treatments failed to help, Jennifer turned to food for healing. Removing grain, dairy and refined sugars and eating "predominantly Paleo," she started reclaiming her life, one whole-food meal at a time. As a wife and mother of three, Jennifer hopes to instill healthy habits in her children now in hopes of creating wellness for a lifetime.

INDEX